Dear Mom:

Remembering, Celebrating, Healing

D0033686

Celebrate
the journey!

Denee

BY DEE DEE RAAP

Reader Reviews

"As a pastor, I walk with those who have lost their mothers to help them do the tender work of grieving, reconciliation, healing, and closure. This book offers a proven, yet simple process of healing available to everyone: simply writing to remember and connect. Dear Mom shows us how to heal by moving from despair to acceptance to joy. Grab the tissue, as you'll cry, and laugh, first at Dee Dee's stories, then, at your own as joyful memories flood your mind."

Rev. Janet Forbes, Denver, CO

"What a gift! Anyone who has lost their mother will relate to the shocking numbness and depression that engulfs you. Dear Mom is a salute to all moms who share their legacies in simple and often unknown ways. Journey with the author as she celebrates the gold nuggets of wisdom she discovered through narrative healing."

Kim Woods, CEO, Kimball, NE

"The world needs this message. If you still have the opportunity to tell someone you love how much they mean to you, tell them. Tell them now. Ask the questions that Dee Dee is now wanting answers to. You will be glad you did."

Renée Middleton, Cheyenne, WY

"I enjoyed going through the healing journey with Dee Dee. Each letter made me realize how much I have taken my own mother for granted. I hadn't finished the book before I sat down and wrote my own mom a letter. Thanks, Dee Dee, for reminding me how important it is to say 'thank you' and 'I love you' before it is too late."

Lynn Vosler, Julesburg, CO

"A superb achievement...Dee Dee Raap has written a book on women from a personal perspective, a unique contribution to life from childhood to motherhood to leaving a legacy. Engaging to read!"

Deanna Trowbridge, Sidney, NE

Dear Mom:

Remembering, Celebrating, Healing

Betty Hauge
May 3, 1928 – December 5, 1990

Disclaimer:
The information contained in this book is intended for
general reference purposes only. It is not a substitute for
professional advice. Guidelines and strategies are meant to
acquaint you with procedures currently available and the
manner in which they can be carried out.

Edited by Caron B. Goode
Layout by Jessica Raap Johnson
Front cover design by Bobbi Lynn Gaukel
Printed and bound by Sioux Printing

Published by JW Press
4015 S. Brady Court
Sioux Falls, SD 57103
605-371-2299
DeeDeeRaap.com

Dedication

To the loving memory of my mother
Betty Hauge

To my daughters
Jessica and Kelsey

Thanks for a wonderful journey!

Acknowledgements

A work like *Dear Mom: Remembering, Celebrating, Healing,* is the result of support and love from many friends and family. Thanks to my friends, whose love and support I count as one of life's great gifts. Special thanks to Diane, who encouraged me from the beginning, to Renee, who shared both ideas and raw courage, and to Virginia, for her faith and wisdom and willingness to read. Thank you to Barbara Aragon, whose words "narrative healing" aptly described the effect the letters to Mom had on my life. Special thanks to Elaine who introduced me to Caron, my editor who has become my friend, who helped turn raw letters of healing into a journey of remembering and celebrating. To my family, Kim, Jessica, and Kelsey, who waited patiently, encouraged tirelessly, and whose love supported the creation of *Dear Mom: Remembering, Celebrating, Healing,* a special thank you.

In addition, to my late mom and dad, my brother, sisters, aunts, uncles and the many wonderful people whose hearts began and remain in a small, rural community in northeastern South Dakota, thank you. It truly has been a wonderful journey!

Table of Contents

Foreword

THE MOTHER-DAUGHTER RELATIONSHIP

The mother-daughter duo is one of the most powerful forces of the human experience. The physical bond and psychological connections developed between mother and daughter create strong feelings and memories that rise above separation, in life and also after the death of one or the other. Even animal research confirms this power of the mother-daughter bond, which during infancy and early childhood can modulate gene expression, neurotransmitter activity, and the hormonal pattern of the stress response. My medical practice, which cares for thousands of mothers and daughters, affirms the lasting formative and transformative impact of this relationship.

Dee Dee and her mother, Betty, model the ideal for women. By reading Dee Dee's story and letters, each reader may identify with her feelings and memories, especially those that develop around hearth and home–the domain of females since ancient times. Through Dee Dee's humorous, inspiring, and heart-wrenching letters, women may smile, laugh, cry and ache as they reflect on their own mother-daughter experiences. The mystery of the mother, an important theme in the mother-daughter duo, is shared in a sensitive letter, "Driving Mrs. Betty." Secrets shared and secrets kept often are a source of conflict and confusion for mothers and daughters, and this book may propel daughters into a process of discovery that leads to realizing and accepting their mothers' vulnerabilities.

Dear Mom: Remembering, Celebrating, Healing portrays the many facets of communication and connections between two women. It is a tribute to the healing capacity of journaling. I personally benefited from Dee Dee sharing her journey through her letters to her mother, and I highly recommend this book to all women. It is a heart-warming affirmation of mothers' ability to instill in their daughters the timeless qualities of compassion, service, love of beauty, courage, and faith, just as Dee Dee's mother graciously portrayed and so artfully nurtured in her daughter.

Kenna Stephenson, M.D.

Author of *Awakening Athena: Resilience, Restoration, and Rejuvenation for Women*

Associate Professor and Scholar in Residence in The College of Nursing and Health Sciences, The University of Texas at Tyler

Assistant Professor of Family Medicine, The University of Texas Health Center at Tyler

Professor of Health Psychology and Behavioral Medicine, Northcentral University, Prescott, AZ

Introduction

The experience of losing a parent in death is almost universal,
and yet many who feel this loss for the first time
are surprised at how painful it can be.
Even those well into adulthood are often taken aback
by the deep sense of loneliness, the sense of being "orphaned,"
that the death of a mother or father can bring.[1]

Reverend Richard Gilbert

Healing from the death of someone you cherish can be a painful process, especially when the special soul dies suddenly. You lose a vital connection, as a life support system, and the result is feeling like an orphan, no matter what your age.

When this happened to me, I knew that I was dying inside because I felt the time bomb going off inside of me ever so slowly. Tick... tick... tick...

A telephone call from my younger sister Gayle on that fateful day of December 5, 1990, changed my life.

"Dee Dee, the hospital just called, they don't think that Mom is going to make it. You'd better get home right away," she begged as she hung up very quickly. Stunned, I called back immediately, only to have her repeat the message with even more urgency.

I was in the midst of the chaos of a kitchen remodeling job in our house, and my only seat was a bucket turned upside down on the kitchen floor. In shock, I sat on the bucket and called my brother. I couldn't think clearly. My husband Kim was traveling for work, I had two small children, and I had to get home.

The phone rang a second time, not five minutes later. Gayle called again to say that Mom did not make it. She had died suddenly of a heart attack. That was the beginning of my journey as a 34-year-old orphan.

THE SHOCK

Emptiness is the feeling I use to describe emotional numbness. Friends shared their words for loss as hollow heart, orphan, abandoned, angry, meaninglessness, or distressing. All of these are true when we lose a loved one, especially when the passing is sudden. Whether our bond is through blood, marriage, or friendship, a human heart that shares such love with another is set adrift on a shoreless wave, riding endlessly until the numbness subsides. The shift from emotional pain back to the land of the living can be foggy. Some people seem able to command their mind and body to walk out of the fog and continue with life. Others stay numbed in pain for a while. The point is that we share the same hollow heart when we lose a loved one, and we all will recover in varying degrees.

NARRATIVE HEALING

I have finally restored my wholeness through a process called narrative healing; I journeyed back through my life with my mother by writing her a series of letters, beginning nine years after her death. This writing method healed the emptiness and was a phenomenal personal journey through time and memories.

Narrative healing works like this: when our pain is too great, the human psyche has remarkable ways to compartmentalize the intense pain, hence the numbness or other coping mechanisms. In the resilience of our human spirit, an inner knowing determines, at some point, that we can handle the grief and the pain now. This ability to handle the grieving happens automatically in this writing process, like slowly opening the door to the heart again. Then the heart says, "Okay, look at the memories, smell the freshly baked chocolate chip cookies, taste the sweet homemade ice cream, listen to the music together, and feel the love again."

Narrative healing allows your heart to open. The truth is that our resilience is directly dependent upon facing the hurt, feeling the vulnerability, and accepting it—all the pain and joy combined—until we don't know whether we are laughing or crying. We move through all the pent up emotions and arrive at a place of acceptance. Acceptance doesn't mean that we don't still feel the pain. It does imply that we can equally choose to know the depth of love and remember the good things, even demand, and claim them, from our memories.

THE DESTINATION

Arriving at this destination of acceptance and healing is a freedom that I want to share with you. *Dear Mom: Remembering, Celebrating, Healing,* is an honest journey through memories that we all have, sequenced in the progress of a healing heart and arriving at the desire to live fully again. My form of narrative was a series of letters to Mom depicting my journey. It is my greatest wish that my narrative healing serve you in this way:

- Help you heal after the loss of a parent or another loved one.

- Offer you a way of saying goodbye.

- Offer you a way of connecting to your own past and your own stories.

- Respect your past and the memories of your loved one as I did mine through honoring my mother and her gifts to me.

- Help you understand that no matter how bad life is, there are gifts of good in it. Your job is to dig for the gold, the true meaning of the experience.

Know that the gold, the wisdom and values in our past, derive from our connections. We connect to our past and to our future through people. My journey of narrative healing began as a series of letters I wrote to my mom nine years after her death. I hope my journey gives you a laugh and a memory of your own. Mostly, I hope it gives you the chance to write your living mother a letter. Do not wait as I did to say all of these things until it is too late. Life is just too short.

Dee Dee Raap

SECTION ONE

Saying Goodbye

I wanted a perfect ending...
Now, I've learned the hard way that some poems don't rhyme,
and some stories don't have a clear beginning, middle and end.
Life is about not knowing,
having to change, taking the moment,
and making the best of it,
without knowing what's going to happen next.
Delicious ambiguity.[2]

Gilda Radner

CHAPTER ONE

The Winter

Those who contemplate the beauty of the earth
find reserves of strength
that will endure as long as life lasts.
There is something infinitely healing
in the repeated refrains of nature-
the assurance that dawn comes after night,
and spring after winter.[3]

Rachel Carson

Winters in South Dakota are beautiful with fluffy snowflakes and fields of white that invite you to cross-country ski or snowmobile and suck in chilled air to rejuvenate your vitality. Snow is delightful or dreary in the winter months. The raging artic wind descends from the North and creates blizzard conditions with blinding snow and wind chill factors that can dip to 86 degrees below zero, a temperature I experienced in December 1984. Sometimes, I think of winter as a time when nothing can live, surely a time of death.

At the time of Mom's death, my family and I were living in Pierre, South Dakota, about 200 miles from my hometown of Roslyn, where my parents Betty and Orville Hauge had lived. In my beautiful family, my husband Kim and my daughters Jessica and Kelsey provided the nurturing support that helped me survive my mother's death. Orphaned like me were my loving siblings: my older brother and two younger sisters. Despite the caring bond we hold, I do not have my mom, and I wish I did.

The first Christmas after Mom died, I attended a Lutheran church service on Christmas Eve. We picked up the *Lutheran Book of Worship*, preparing to sing. The last song of the service, entitled, "I'm So Glad Each Christmas Eve," includes these words in verse five, "When mother trims the tree each year which fills the room with light...." I had never seen that hymn in my life even though I'd been a Lutheran for a number of years. The refrain grated my raw feelings, and I ran out of church crying. The time bomb went off.

This is how grief hits, a silent tsunami rising, seeking the shore of release. The last time I saw Mom she was in her casket. My mind reeled from the lack of closure. I couldn't talk to her. I missed her. I never said goodbye. Her death denied me those conversations that I'd have had if I'd known our time together was limited. Without those conversations, I felt deprived of any opportunity to heal. Mom was just gone, and her absence left hollowness, a huge empty hole. Nothing fills the hollow space, except perhaps a journey through time.

A JOURNEY OF MEMORIES

Dear Mom,

A journey of memories is one of the best parts of life. Journeys back in time to recall joyfully the events, moments, and activities that shaped us. A journey to a time that seemed simpler and less complicated, when you were the mom, and I was your daughter.

That's what this series of letters is all about, Mom. Your life was cut short. You died December 5, 1990, at age 62. I was only 34, and I left many things unsaid because there was not enough time. Even 34 years wasn't enough time.

These letters are a way of saying that I hope you are still listening because I have so much to tell you. I hope you enjoy the journey of memories and the place where I am at today, much to your credit, Mom. That's a compliment!

Love,

Dee Dee

I was haunted for years by not being able to say goodbye. The letters I wrote to my mom were important communication tools for my healing. All of my life, the written word facilitated my healing and helped me develop the resilience for difficult situations. Poems, essays, journals—I have written countless pages over my life, reflecting and growing through the process of writing. This form of narrative healing finally filled the hollow hole.

MEMORIES OF CHRISTMAS PAST

Dear Mom,

I sit on my couch next to the Christmas tree in our home in Cheyenne and look at the ornaments that you made for us. I realized that it has been nine years since I had Christmas with you. That's a long time. Your sudden, unexpected death just before the holiday was hard on me. I've spent years being unable to enjoy the spirit of the holiday again. This year, I have felt festive and more alive than any Christmas since you died.

You made dozens of ornaments for us, Mom, and every year, they adorn the tree. Crocheted snowflakes; cross-stitched bird feeders, complete with bird and bird food; beaded angels; and cross-stitched mailboxes, eager for Christmas cards from afar.

Even the ornaments on my tree that you didn't make remind me of you: small stuffed animals in whimsical colors, festive Hallmark balls that date each year of my daughters' lives, candy cane decorations handmade by your granddaughters.

You kept the pleasures of life simple, Mom. You took the simple ingredients of crafts and made them sparkle for my tree. Every year I open the box of ornaments, regard them with love, hold them with care, and place them on the tree in remembrance of you and the way you loved Christmas.

I still cherish the early Christmas celebrations on the farm in South Dakota. Remember the plaid dresses that Grandma Weyer made for me to wear? I searched for Santa through Grandma and Grandpa's windows as I heard his sleigh go by, yet being too little to get the same view as my brother. Every year the Weyer cousins performed the Christmas story, wearing capes, holding the baby Jesus and singing Christmas songs.

One year Santa brought me a folding card table and four chairs. That was a marvelous Christmas present! I played on that table and chairs for many hours, serving tea to stuffed animals and an occasional sibling.

The Christmas cookies you made every year smelled so delicious—cut-outs, perfectly baked, and then frosted in red, green, and white. Santa's bells, trees baked to holiday perfection. Sweet date cookies rolled in coconut make my mouth water. Jubilee Jumbles. And thumb print cookies that looked nice but were way too adult for me to enjoy.

Baking sugar cookies is on my list of things to do today, Mom. First, I just wanted to sit, enjoy a cup of coffee on my couch, and look at our tree. It may have been a decade since I've had a Christmas with you, but I know you are here with us, through your ornaments, through your love for my children, and through the customs of Christmas that I took for granted as a child. Thank you for the ornaments and traditions, Mom. They make my Christmas special.

Merry Christmas Mom!

Mom left her heart behind in many ways. Healing was about looking back, finding the good in my mother's life, and celebrating those memories. The Christmas tree in my living room was the starting point for that because I'd looked at what Mom had made and realized how much she gave me in my 34 years with her. I saw everything anew that Christmas, and found so much good. That was the start of my healing—remembering, and even celebrating, the good.

CHRISTMAS MUSIC

Dear Mom,

Christmas music brings you to my thoughts because I remember when we got the phonograph and our first albums— Nat King Cole, Jim Reeves and Bing Crosby.

For being raised on a farm in the northeastern corner of South Dakota, we enjoyed great diversity in musical tastes. The message and comfort from the familiar songs is meaningful to me even today.

The world keeps changing, Mom. Today's music is very different from what we had, and yet I find myself playing the same music we had on the farm. It's comforting to hear those tunes now with my children. It took me years to find the old Jim Reeves' Christmas album, and I was like a happy little kid when I did. We spent hours listening to it as we decorated the tree, made the cookies, and wrapped the presents.

One of the lines I like best on the Jim Reeves' album is, "...Soon it will be Christmas Day." So much preparation goes into the holiday, and then suddenly, here it is. I am sure you felt the same way, especially with all the baking you did. Tonight I am baking the same date cookies you used to make for us. No one in my household likes them, but I love them. It's my way of keeping your memory alive, Christmas after Christmas.

Mom, soon it will be Christmas Day. Another Christmas without you, but I find you everywhere I turn, so I think you are here after all.

Merry Christmas Mom!

Chapter Two

By Hand

Love is, above all, the gift of oneself.

Jean Anouilh

In our lives on the South Dakota prairie, each object we make is an expression of our hearts. Love goes into what we do, whether it's decorating a Christmas tree or creating a gift for another. The memories and gifts from my past are my treasures today.

Today, I honor Mom's round crocheted doily by showcasing it in a round oak frame that hangs on the wall next to the antique oak secretary. Crocheting and knitting were functional art forms that little fingers like mine did not master easily. Women crocheted fast, and they were coordinated. My little fingers tried, but took up knitting instead. Two needles seemed easier. The proof that I know how to knit rests in an antique trunk; that blue turtleneck sweater looked great on the cover of the knitting magazine. Enough said. I just can't throw it out. My daughters are going to want to wear it some day, I'm sure.

BY MOM'S HANDS

Dear Mom,

The day you died, you were finishing a beautiful, rose-colored afghan for Kelsey. I found it next to your chair. You must have spent hours on it, sitting in your brown recliner, that cozy spot ten feet from the TV that broadcast the soap operas you loved so well.

Aunt Florence finished the afghan. Both Jessie and Kelsey have an afghan made by you, and they treasure that precious gift of your time, Mom.

I remember making one for you when Kim and I had our first Christmas as a married couple. We lived at the state park the summer after we were married, and my job as a gate attendant meant hours of doing nothing. So, I knitted, and I knitted. I knitted a gold afghan for Kim's mom, and the green and yellow one for you.

Knitting afghans was one way of honoring you for all that you made for us over the years. You sewed all of our clothes. Do you remember the green plaid coat with its perfect topstitching? Then there were the blue plaid skirt with attached suspenders, and the cotton blouses, shorts, and dresses. We never bought clothes in a store, and only occasionally did we order slacks from the Sears Roebuck catalog.

At the time, I didn't realize we were too poor to shop for store-bought clothes. I assumed every mom made every daughter's clothes. I understood it was different for boys. You didn't sew pants for Rick as you did for me, but he was a boy, so that was okay.

I learned from you that if we wanted clothes, we had to sew them. I learned to sew dresses, blouses, and shirts. I remember sewing the red skirt and jacket that I needed for Future Homemakers of America because I was a state officer. The topstitch thread was a challenge with the size of needle we had on the machine. You taught me to go as far as I could and finish the rest by hand.

By hand is how life was on the farm and in the small town of Roslyn, South Dakota. We hemmed, knitted and baked food from scratch because you taught us to enjoy our achievements and value our talents.

Your hands, Mom, made so many things for us. Those long fingers must have grown tired from your long days. I cherish those memories Mom, and I am sorry it took me so many years to appreciate your efforts.

Love,

Dee Dee

Mom taught us to create and share whatever delights our handscrafted. Even brownies! One day, Mom encouraged me to share my brownie with my sister and told me to cut it with a knife, but my sister would have first choice of pieces. Perplexed, I finally caught on. I had to cut the brownie into equal parts, or I wouldn't get—nor give—my fair share. Mom was more than "fair and sharing" in the cutting and preparing of food. Like many women of the prairie, whenever a social event occurred at church or school, Mom showed up with food. One of the best things Mom's hands ever made was her homemade pies.

PIES MADE FROM SCRATCH

Dear Mom,

Do you remember your delicious pies? You made the crust and the filling from scratch. People rarely do that any more. They buy the crust from Pillsbury and the filling from Wilderness. They put them together and call it homemade pie because it didn't come out of the freezer.

My big brother Rick used to make the graham cracker crust for your vanilla custard pie whenever you went to town. He knew that if you saw the crust when you returned from town, you wouldn't waste it. Of course, you would make the vanilla custard to go into the crust. That was such a delicious pie!

We grew apples on Grandma's farm. An apple orchard just behind the house provided the Weyers and the Hauges with many apple desserts, but the pies were always the best. Grandma used to peel the entire apple into one long strip of peel for me. I've never been able to duplicate that feat to impress my own kids.

You were a bit of a holdout on your apple pies, though

Mom. Dad loved apple pie. However, you told him you couldn't make apple pies from Delicious apples, the only kind available in the grocery stores in the winter.

Dad only had apple pie in the summer. Imagine Dad's surprise when someone told him that she used Delicious apples to make pies year-round. You were sneaky, Mom. That trick saved you from making apple pies during the winter for at least the first 20 years of your marriage.

A friend told me that his wife made homemade pies with homemade fillings to sell for a charity event. She had made 120 pies and sold them for $5. My mouth drooled. My second thought after the taste was that she could have gotten $10 apiece, easy, for homemade crust and homemade filling. Gee Mom, you could have gotten rich making and selling your homemade pies!

Love,

Dee Dee

The rich traditions of rolling out pie dough, knitting an afghan, or sharing a cup of hot chocolate while Jim Reeves sings our favorite carols are the memories that a mother creates for her children. Maybe family life on the prairie is really about creating funny and tender memories of traditions for each other.

MERRY CHRISTMAS MOM

Dear Mom,

December 25, 1999 is the last Christmas of the decade, the century, and the millennium. This Christmas marks the end of any Christmas followed by "19___." I wonder how "Christmas 2000" looks on letterhead.

Christmas is here, Mom, and love is in the air. We're on our way to see Dad and the rest of my family. Your children's families are maturing, Mom. Last night, Jessie, Kelsey, and their cousins reminisced past Christmases and how Santa arrived in the house. They are sure they saw him one night, even past the age of disbelief. They recalled how they had asked Santa for a small doll and got an expensive camera instead, and said, "That's not what I asked Santa for!"

When we left Cheyenne for our trip to South Dakota, we forgot Jessie and Kelsey's Christmas stockings that still hang by the fireplace with care. The girls got creative and rescued dirty socks from their suitcases. You just can't take a chance with Santa on Christmas Eve!

Christmas is a time of memories: making memories, recalling memories, and telling stories to carry on the memories.

Keeping your memory alive is one of my Christmas goals, Mom. Maybe I can't let go of you. Perhaps I think my daughters need to know you as I did: a creative woman who fashioned gifts out of next to nothing; a woman who never criticized them and spent her time making things with them.

When we visited Grandma's, the girls went directly to the back bedroom to get out the crafts because they knew you would help them. Cross-stitching yarn on plastic canvas entertained Jessie for hours, bonded the two of you, and taught her the joy of creative hands.

I haven't done much of that with them, Mom. Did I do it with you? I remember knitting with my aunts and Grandma Olga. I think you do this task with another woman besides your mom. Maybe it has to do with time and patience. A grandma is supposed to have the time and patience to make things, solve problems, and listen. I hope to be that kind of grandmother.

You would love to see your granddaughters today, Mom. You would be proud, and they would talk your ear off. Of course, that could interfere with your soap operas. Then, today is Christmas, no soaps today, just Christmas music, Christmas stories, and Christmas love shared between a grandmother and her granddaughters.

Love,

Dee Dee

Our families got through Christmas without Mom by cherishing the traditions, recipes, the ornaments, and crafts. Several generations sharing stories together provided the warm camaraderie that other family members and I needed. Yet, no matter how comforting we were for each other, our hearts still felt a little sting whenever we faced another departure, loss, or goodbye.

THE ACT OF DEPARTING

Dear Mom,

Jessie is now 19 and leaving for college soon. It seems that the upcoming departure has brought out the best in her. Yesterday at church, she held my hand during one of the choir's performances. She gave me some of her best artwork, and she's done whatever tasks I ask her help with in the kitchen.

Does the act of departing bring out the best in us? Maybe when we realize that time is finite, we transform our behavior into the best it can be. When we no longer assume "forever" exists, we appreciate and value that which we have.

Jessie said she would miss me because I make her laugh. She can't believe some of the things I say. Guess I've become "off the wall" in my view of life and have developed the ability to say what I wish without concern for how the words land.

You taught me in an extremely hard way that "forever" doesn't exist. I assumed I would have a mother for many more years, or that my daughters would have a grandmother for graduations, weddings, and to hold their babies as you had held mine. Assumptions made me take you for granted.

I am sorry, Mom. I wish I hadn't taken you for granted. I wish I had sat down with you many more days and just talked, visited, and learned more about you. I want to know why you became a teacher, and if you missed it when you became a housewife and mother. I wish I knew why you baked what you did, chose the colors in clothes and decorating. I wonder what your life was like as a little girl on the farm and how you and Dad fell in love.

You were always there for me. Then one day, you were not. Now I try to answer the questions through my own experiences with my daughters. I think I am beginning to understand.

Thanks Mom!

SECTION TWO

A Memorable Journey

*The secret of health for both mind and body
is not to mourn for the past,
worry about the future,
or anticipate troubles
but to live in the present moment
wisely and earnestly.*

Buddha

CHAPTER THREE

Great Memories

Know that every single moment
of anything remotely good
is a gift.

Julia Roberts

When the one you love has passed on, your heart floods you with feelings and pictures. These memory flashbacks can run in the early morning hours. They can sneak in through different doorways:

- When your body is busy and the mind has a free moment to open the door of memories.

- When you take a break for a hot cup of coffee, and a rush of emotions overwhelms you.

- When you sink into a relaxing hot tub and tears wet your eyes.

Yes, the recollections pop up from nowhere with a giant crayon to color your world blue. When they colored my world "sad and shocked" for so many years, I allowed them entry. The memories, even the most painful, reminded me that I am alive and well and in charge of my life. I captured them in writing with the narrative healing process. The recollections brought forth the pain and poignancy. From those I started reclaiming the good times—the gold of my life with Mom.

DREAMS

Dear Mom,

After you died, I had several dreams about you, and often woke up startled and frightened. In one dream, you were a young mom on the farm, and I was trying hard to warn you about something dangerous "out there." In another dream, you turned into an old, haggard mom, about 20 years beyond your age at death. The dreams frightened me because you talked to me and it felt like you were right there. I finally woke up from one dream and told myself it was okay; all I had to do was listen to you. I did finally. The message from you, repeatedly, was that all was okay. You were okay, I was okay, and it was all okay. I took comfort in that message, despite the agonizing grief I felt. You were talking to me and that was comforting.

Are you still talking to me? Are you still there, watching over me, guiding me?

I don't know if people we love here on earth become our guardian angels, but I don't doubt it. I have been on a spiritual journey ever since you died, and I am sure that is not coincidental either.

If you are my angel, or my daughters' angel, I thank you. I know you cared so much for us and loved us dearly. I know you didn't say that, but you felt it. It makes sense to me that you are having a very busy afterlife watching over us, caring for us, loving us. And if you're not? Well, that's okay, too. I just think you would make a great angel!

Love,

Dee Dee

Whether on earth or in heaven, perhaps mothers serve as the angelic watch guards all of our lives. Even a grandmother still watches her middle-aged daughter for growth and change, even as she indulges her grandchildren. If your Mom is your angel, perhaps you might write her a letter with some of your earliest memories and gratitude. These are the cherished memories that I celebrated.

EARLIEST MEMORIES

Dear Mom,

Earliest memories tell about experiences of the sweetest kind, when bodies were small, life was simple, and impressions were huge.

Mom, my earliest memory is with your dad on his farm. As the crow flies, our home was only one mile from Grandma and Grandpa's. However, going via road meant a three-mile drive, a long distance in those days.

Your youngest sister, Aunt Gennie, reminds me that I was very special to Grandpa. In fact, I think she would say he spoiled me. In a typical farm visit, I watched Grandma Weyer make pies, and I fell down the steps and played in Grandpa's hayloft. I used the outhouse in which catalog paper made the experience even more authentic. I don't know how many hours I spent on Grandpa's farm, but these early memories are plentiful.

Grandpa farmed with workhorses—big, huge, tall horses that pulled the farm implements. He plowed and he hauled hay with those massive horses that were a critical part of farming.

When I was about three years old, Grandpa carved a shotgun for me. He whittled a piece of wood into a gun for his tomboy granddaughter. I wish I still had that gun because it meant the world to me, and I carried it so proudly, aiming carefully and shooting at nothing.

I always wanted to stay overnight at Grandma and Grandpa's. But every time I stayed, I would get homesick in the middle of the night. Grandpa would have to throw on his shoes, fire up the old Ford, and drive me home. He always said, "Yes."

Gennie was still living at home when I was little. I remember sleeping with her in her upstairs bedroom that was directly over Grandma and Grandpa's room. One night in particular, Gennie discouraged letting me stay because I never actually spent the entire night. Very logical, of course, but Grandpa let me stay. Sure as the rooster crowing at dawn, I woke up in the middle of the night and wanted to go home. Gennie hollered through the furnace vent to Grandma, who told her to tell me to go back to sleep. However, I was insistent, and Grandpa got up and took me home once again.

Wasn't that special? I felt so incredibly welcomed, loved, and tenderly cared for. The best apple pies in the world, horses to ride, guns to shoot. The world of Grandma and Grandpa's farm was sweet. What a great place for my earliest memories.

Love,

Dee Dee

When I wrote my Mom letters, I wondered about her earliest memories. I don't have many mementos or photographs of her early life. Most of what I know came from the stories told by Dad, aunts and uncles and my brother in family gatherings or telephone calls. And the stories just made me smile.

THE WEDDING

Dear Mom,

Fifty-one years ago today on January 4, two moms of different ethnic backgrounds and religions watched their children marry. The day started with a blizzard that the mothers might have called "divine intervention." However, the weather cleared, and my determined father drove through blowing snow and harsh winds to marry the woman he loved.

Not only was the world full of routine 51 years ago, it was simpler. In our corner of South Dakota, people were Norwegians, Swedes, or Germans. A few were from Yugoslavia or Czechoslovakia, and they all were Lutheran or Catholic. We knew nothing of blacks, Asians or Jews. Our ancestors' countries and religions defined who we were, and we simply accepted that definition of ourselves.

Dad's side of our family was Norwegian Lutheran, and your side was German Catholic. The two of you had the nerve to fall in love. What did the mothers think? I doubt they were pleased. After all, you couldn't marry in the Catholic Church because you were marrying a heathen Lutheran. Both of you broke the rules. I know Dad's sister Bernice always liked you, Mom. But Grandma? That may have been another story.

Back then, our corner of the world evolved around ethnic groups that immigrated to America and settled in South Dakota. While those differences seem minor today, they were significant then. The two faiths were not equal, many said, and church laws reflected that. They didn't marry "interfaith," and I'm not so sure that they welcomed the mixing of heritages either.

Aunt Bernice gave me one picture of you and Dad cutting your wedding cake outside. The snow in the background was the perfect frame for the January 4th wedding and the reception which was held on the farm the next day. This picture is one of my cherished possessions. You and Dad looked very happy 51 years ago, interfaith marriage or not.

Love,

Dee Dee

Half a century later, we do not give so much thought to mixed marriages of faiths or ethnicity. There has been a natural progression of acceptance as more immigrants of many ethnic mixtures come to the United States. However, each of us still holds our heritage and customs dear to our hearts.

ETHNIC SOUTH DAKOTA

Dear Mom,

Today, I work as a training and marketing consultant and motivational speaker. I am blessed to have the opportunity to influence people. I help them see the possibilities in themselves and help them acquire or enhance their skills. I feel honored to be doing this, and I have great fun in the process.

One reason that I enjoy it so much is that I've become a storyteller. I tell stories from my life to help people see that if I can be successful, so can they.

I tell a particular story about growing up in ethnic South Dakota to people in my customer service training. I emphasize the point that we grow up in situations and do not realize until a later time exactly how that situation influenced our beliefs and perceptions. I had no idea I grew up in such an ethnic world. Rather, it is more accurate to say I had no idea that not everybody else in the world grew up in similar environments. Our world was so small that I assumed everyone else was like us.

Three towns formed the borders of my childhood and the foundations of our ethnic traditions. Roslyn was Scandinavian Lutheran; Grenville was Polish Catholic; and Eden was German Catholic. What kinds of jokes did we tell in those days, Mom? Ethnic jokes! Remember all the Norwegian jokes and the

Swedish jokes? If we were all feeling brave, we would even tell a German Catholic joke, but not very often. It seems that even we had some boundaries, even then.

Telling ethnic jokes was a part of our every day world because there was no malice, only humor. If you told one, you expected one in return. The absence of the return joke was a let down. The exchange and bantering was fun and we did it well.

One of our favorite television shows was the hit sitcom, All in the Family. *Do you remember that show, Mom? We laughed at Archie Bunker, felt sorry for Edith, and wondered about the dizzy daughter, Gloria. Then there was Meathead. I laughed right along with Archie as he told Polish jokes. Remember our amazement the night Meathead told Archie to stop the jokes, that he didn't appreciate them? I wondered as a child what was wrong with him. Why wouldn't he like Polish jokes since he was Polish? Had he lost his sense of humor?*

As I grew older, I realized what the phrase "politically correct" meant, although that was years before the public used that phrase. Today it is just not politically correct to tell ethnic jokes. However, it's still a way of honoring each other back there in ethnic South Dakota.

Love,

Dee Dee

Such are my reminiscences of humor and family jokes. When my childlike eyes perceived those situations in childhood that contributed to my stockpile of golden memories, I wrote them down. The narratives unlocked the appreciation for my culture, and reminded me how I became an avid sports fan, an important part of who I am today.

BEING 10

Dear Mom,

A devotional reading this morning encouraged me to recall being 10 years old. According to the author, that was the last time I trusted my instincts and lived as my "authentic self." I took a close look at my authenticity.

At age 10, I was in fourth or fifth grade, tall, and skinny. You were probably telling me to be grateful for being tall on one of those days when I hurried off the school bus in tears over merciless teasing.

You tried to make me feel better by pointing out a future advantage, but I couldn't relate. I didn't care about being able to reach the top cupboard someday. Of course, you were right. Today I do care, and it is a great advantage.

At age 10, I played with Barbie, and that meant one thing: fighting with my sister. We had a simple way of solving differences. Gayle hit me on the head with the Barbie doll when she got tired of my bossing her around. When we really fought, we would get physical, at least she would. She was stronger than I was, and would land on top quickly. It never helped that I would get the giggles and laugh. I just couldn't take it seriously, so I laughed and giggled, giving her an unfair advantage. Or so I thought. I am not sure she would agree, but it was authentic!

I do recall an important event at age 10. My brother Rick was 14 and a great sports fan. He collected every New York Yankee baseball card, and he watched pitchers voraciously. He, too, was a pitcher, and worked hard at it. On the farm, he threw the baseball into the hay bales stacked against the barn, over and over again.

Sometimes I would throw the ball back. However, his usual

routine was to walk to the barn, pick up the ball, walk back to the homemade pitcher's mound, and throw it again. He must have been either incredibly patient or incredibly bored!

Rick was also a football fan of a dominant 1960's football team that he worshipped. It was a miraculous moment for a mere 10-year-old child when Rick looked at me and said, "Thou shalt be a Green Bay Packer fan." I shrugged and said, "Okay." What did I know?

I had done everything else my big brother told me to do: trapping muskrats, grabbing the electric fence, and catching a gunnysack full of frogs for Johnny's bait shop in Roslyn.

At age 10, I became a Packer fan. Being a real die-hard meant reading a story in Reader's Digest *about Green Bay's great quarterback, Bart Starr, entitled, "Bart Starr: Nice Guy Finishes First." It meant seeing the results of Lombardi's commitment to excellence on every level, and understanding the desire to win. The message was clear: give life your best shot, every day. It was an incredibly powerful message, one that I wish every 10-year-old could hear.*

So being 10 was good, I would say. Barbies, swimming in Pickeral Lake and watching the Packers win the first Super Bowl. Life doesn't get much better than that!

Love,

Dee Dee

Then again, life did get better as I got older. The more I write, the more I feel that I was as authentic as any 10 year-old can be. Mom's passing has helped me to be even more so. When you realize the brevity of life, you become

bolder, almost fearless, a'
you remember yourself
golden nuggets of m

Success at A

Dear Mom,

    I think growing up on the jᵤ
were sheltered. Rick didn't allow me tᵤ
were a long ways from Main Street and the .
town that had 256 residents. I trusted everyone. ᵤ
of this was my belief that anything was possible. I plaу
believe with my imaginary friend, Jane. I trusted Dad's storιᵤ
and thought that if I wanted anything, it was always possible.
The imaginary world held countless possibilities, and I believed
them all achievable.

    Around age 10, Santa brought me a red plastic cash register
with rows of numbers. Its tray popped out, just like the real ones.
I loved playing store. It was a challenge, though, because I did not
have very many customers.

    One day I decided that I would have a lemonade stand.
Remember that hot sunny day, Mom? I created a lemonade stand
using my bronze table, lemonade-for-sale sign, and my cash
register. I opened the garage door and was ready for business.

    I think you and Dad bought the first glass. I was so proud. I
knew it would be a great success. We were about 35 yards from a
dusty gravel road. The same road the school bus drove every day.
The same road that led to church, town, relatives, or anywhere we
went.

    What luck! The road construction crew moved in that hot

ob was to get the road ready to cover with
saw my sign and wanted my lemonade, but not
ey brought Thermos containers to fill with
lemonade stand was a great success!

it would work, but I have always wondered one thing.
many gallons of lemonade did you and Rick actually
n that hot kitchen as I kept ringing up the totals on my
register? Mom, did I share the proceeds? I'll have to buy
k a glass of lemonade on his next visit in memory of a very
ot day and a very successful lemonade stand in northeastern
South Dakota!

Love,

Dee Dee

At this point, the narrative healing shifts from the nostalgia of losing my mother to the joy of uncovering humorous and fun moments. I should christen this writing process as Narrative Celebrations. There is no way that your unconscious, socked-away grief and emptiness can hide as you write. Your attention to the journey through memories absolutely invites those hidden nuggets to surface. They pop up into your head just grinning at you, waving their little arms, and screaming, "Write me down! I'll make you laugh. Choose me!" Writing letters makes you smile, and that changes your attitude for the better.

CHAPTER FOUR

Nostalgia

Nostalgia is like a grammar lesson:
you find the present tense,
but the past perfect!

Owens Lee Pomeroy

Nostalgia implies that when I write passages in my narrative journal, a mixture of feelings arise. If I recall homesickness from my past, I ask myself, "What healing does this bring me?" If memories fill me with joy, I celebrate. From all memories, I seek wisdom, which I consider my treasure. Some recollections bring questions whose answers I'll never know. The purpose is the journey and the celebration. The benefits of allowing my heart's well of impressions and textures to bubble up and spill over are:

- To root out all of my memories.
- To censor nothing in order to reveal all.
- To stake my claim on unexplored territory.
- To claim my gold nuggets of wisdom.

Reclaiming and accepting my true past makes me savor the day and relish this moment, sharing with you.

DRIVING MRS. BETTY

Dear Mom,

One thing I never saw you do was drive a vehicle. Every time we went anywhere, Dad drove. I grew up thinking that moms just didn't drive. As I grew older and saw other moms drive, I was confused. It seemed so limiting for you and us that we could only leave the farm if Dad could drive. Your taking us wasn't an option.

As a kid, I wasn't in a hurry to drive. I actually grew up fearful of driving. When I asked why you didn't drive, Dad told me you used to drive until the day you had an accident with me. Apparently I was in the back seat when you were driving and had to hit the brakes. The impact threw me forward and injured my face. I am not sure how bad it was, but it was the last time you drove.

I always felt guilty about that, Mom. It was my fault that you didn't drive and were bound to the farm. You couldn't get away easily. I remember only one time that a friend picked you up to take you some place.

I am sorry, Mom, that you had such a limiting experience with me. It must have really scared you and shaken your confidence. I wish I could go back in time and show you how safe driving is, and sometimes, stuff just happens. It was okay, Mom.

Love,

Dee Dee

Perhaps I could feel Mom's reluctance to drive inside myself, as most children internalize feelings. I often wanted to show her how easy driving could be, to fix her pain in some way. It did not keep me from learning to drive though, in a rather comical scene right out of *Saturday Night Live*.

LEARNING TO DRIVE THE FORD PICKUP

Dear Mom,

My time to learn how to drive arrived on another hot summer day. I was only 14, and Dad was my teacher. That should have been my first clue. Although he was sweet and wonderful, he was not a teacher.

We got into the old, green 1964 Ford pickup, and both of us settled into the seats. Dad showed me the gears by saying "High, Low, Reverse," but the stick shift handle only had the numbers 1, 2, and 3 on it, with R for reverse. I did not know what was high or low. Dad put Sandy, the golden Labrador hunting dog, in the pickup with us, took me to the cornfield of stubble, and told me to drive. He tried unsuccessfully to show me how the clutch worked, and the stick shift numbers confused me. I was excited that I was learning to drive, and my excitement added to the muddled lessons.

Imagine this scene, Mom: there I was, in the pickup with Sandy, in the cornfield stubble, sitting behind the wheel of that old green Ford. I felt good and proud. We bucked so hard when I slipped the clutch that Sandy tried to jump out the window. It is difficult when the family dog wants to abandon you.

I wonder what you thought, Mom. Since you had an accident that injured me, were you afraid for me? I was afraid for me. I was actually 17 before I got my license. I never have been a very confident driver.

Jessie drives, and now it is Kelsey's turn. Now I get to be the mom, watching my daughters learn to drive. At least Kelsey is not in a cornfield with a dog in the passenger seat.

Love,

Dee Dee

My brother Rick was out of the house by the time I got my license to drive, and Mom never commented on my driving. Sometimes over a phone call Rick and I share our best memories of growing up. He reminded me of sleeping on sheets dried on a clothes line in the prairie breeze, and we laughed, as I am sure Downy tried to capture that particular scent. Sleeping on clean, sweet smelling cotton sheets is as good as it gets.

In your own journey through your memories, find a family member who will share their stories to spark your own recollection. Ask good friends to listen and provide their memoirs. The more support and comfort you have while traveling back through time, the easier it is to surrender to the healing process. The more support you have, the more love and comfort you can receive. Even better is the laughter you'll share at the embarrassing and naive moments we all grow through.

THE DANGEROUS ROLLING PIN

Dear Mom,

Some things embarrassed you more than others. Dad was always the great tease, but when I was about seven years old, I didn't realize he was teasing. To me, what Dad said was fact! After all, my Dad had said so. I had no qualms about repeating Dad's stories, and did so easily.

The first time I repeated Dad's stories was when I was in first grade. I told my teacher the story I had heard at home: the bumps on Dad's head were from you hitting him over the head with the rolling pin. And one day when my teacher corrected me for drinking soup out of the bowl, I told her that's how we did it at home.

What I best recall is the look on your face when I told you about those events at school. I think you were more embarrassed about those stories than anything else I did for a long time. At least until I became a teenager!

Love,

Dee Dee

Teasing Uncles

Dear Mom,

I was a lucky kid on the farm because I had uncles who teased me. I didn't count that as a blessing at the time, but it made me feel special, and I sure learned how to take teasing.

You raised an uncle for my kids, Mom. Rick is that uncle today, and he is great. He called tonight to see how Kelsey is doing. Rick genuinely cares, and yet he teases her fiercely. He does the same thing with Jessica.

Why do uncles carry that role? Are they so naturally inclined to tease the children of their sisters? Is it some chemical imbalance? Is it just their way of getting back at their sisters for earlier years of torment?

When your brother, Uncle Gene, visited us, he would do disgusting things like wear my snow boots and tell the world that they fit. I still think he stretched them mechanically before putting HIS big feet into them! Your brother-in-law, Roger, used to call me "Cackle," saying it had to do with the way I laughed.

My uncles are special people in my life. Roger spent a great deal of time with my daughters, carrying on the "uncle" tradition. He teases them about their own stuff, and he teases them about me. After all, how many teenagers have a mother who still responds to "Cackle?"

Probably the biggest tease over the years was Dad. That has to be where Rick got it. Dad teased in a nice way. He never hurt your feelings, but he did know how to make a point or two through teasing. It seemed to be the way of communication, and the generations carry it on.

Love,

Dee Dee

I doubt that most uncles tease with love the way mine did. I think it was the emotional tone of our family and the ability to live closely that allowed the bantering. There is value in learning not to take life so personally, to toughen up a little with resilience by people who love you. Can you remember those who showed their love through teasing?

SOAPS DON'T CHANGE THAT MUCH

Dear Mom,

Some things don't change much over the years. Despite technology, e-mail, satellite transmissions, and wireless cell phones, we still have television soap operas, and kids still watch them.

I admit to precious few people the fact that I watched soaps as a kid. The Guiding Light, *the* Young and the Restless, The Edge of Night. *I remember characters who married, and then, oh my, divorced. I remember Dad coming in from the hay field and asking if Don and Nancy from* The Edge of Night *were getting divorced. We watched those shows religiously during summer vacation with you, but you watched them all year long.*

I like to think I am beyond that now. Give me a good novel, and I am happy. I'd like to assume that my daughters would be more like me, preferring a good book to expand their minds and horizons, broaden their vocabulary, take them to new places, and learn about other cultures.

But what do my kids do when they're home for a sick day during the school year and during summer vacation? They watch soaps! It drives me crazy—the biggest waste of time, and my daughters should be above that. But they are not. They enjoy these daytime serials. They know the characters. They like the stories, the suspense, and the good-looking guys.

Some things don't change, Mom, even though I think they should. Then again, maybe I don't really think they should change. Maybe it is mother like daughter like grandmother.

Love,

Dee Dee

The appearance of prairie life doesn't change quickly, and family heart-felt traditions—even watching soap operas—last through several generations. However, the truer memories that grip our hearts involve stories of endurance and resilience, when sudden changes like fires and tornadoes destroy homes and communities. Such events remind us that we are human and have compassion, and prompt us, yet again, to respect the simplicity of prairie life.

SECTION THREE

Simple Living

Simplicity, clarity, singleness:
these are the attributes
that give our lives
power and vividness and joy.

Richard Holloway

CHAPTER FIVE

The Simpler Ways

Normal day, let me be aware of the treasure you are.
Let me learn from you, love you, bless you before you depart.
Let me not pass you by in quest of some rare and perfect tomorrow.
Let me hold you while I may, for it may not always be so.
One day I shall dig my nails into the earth,
or bury my face in the pillow, or stretch myself taut,
or raise my hands to the sky and want,
more than all the world, your return.

Mary Jean Iron

Simpler ways suggest that prairie living is neither elaborate nor embellished. Our environments shape our lives: harsh winds, swirling dust, migrating waterfowl, reflecting glacial lakes, strong Ponderosa pines, and delicate spring wild flowers. Yet, beneath the veneer of simpler, hearty peoples are complex ecosystems that nourish us.

For example, as outstanding as the snow-sculpted plains in winter are the summer seas of grasses, which consist of three types: tall, short, and mixed. Within the tall grassy pasturelands are the flicker-tail gophers that burrow entire communities and chirp with their personal vocal language. Four-footed creatures such as jackrabbits, coyotes, white-tailed deer, and red fox carry seeds on their fur and disseminate through their waste material. The shorter grasses of the South Dakota plains provide a rougher terrain for hunting owls, slithering snakes, badgers, gophers and other burrowing critters.

So it is within prairie families. Our roots run deep. Beneath the surface of our simpler lives are generational foundations of resilience that provide strength and values. Each subsequent generation can test their mettle against these values and the family foundations.

SIMPLICITY ON THE PRAIRIE

Dear Mom,

When I think of life on the prairie farm, I think of simplicity. We didn't go many places: Pickeral Lake on Sundays, alternating with visits to Grandma and Grandpa's or Aunt Gennie's houses. Town for groceries on rainy summer days or to town via the school bus Monday through Friday was our pattern. Our life was predictable and simple.

When did life got more complicated? When did values

change? When did I notice the complexity? When did I start taking on so much more? Did wanting, having, and doing more come from not having much as a kid and wanting to fill that void? Did it come because I never saw you throw anything away? You were, after all, a Depression kid, which meant you recycled everything, and God forbid if you ever threw anything away.

Whatever the reason, I developed a complicated habit of collecting a lot of things early in my adult life. The acquiring phase lasted a long time. Then, as the prairie seasons, I moved into the shedding phase. Now I try to find good homes for things that I really don't want or need.

Maybe my needs have changed. I don't need stuff any more to define who I am, Mom. "Less is more," describes me now. I like having the time to write, pray, and read. I relish the leisure to sit in my backyard with no real purpose and take the time to share conversation with friends. Stuff just gets in the way of that, so I want less stuff.

Simplicity comes with a price. It is hard to throw away old cards, especially after you taught me the joys of re-reading them later in life. Now, I toss carefully. I keep letters from you, Grandma Olga, and Bernice. I tucked away Jessie's and Kelsey's baby cards and birthday greetings. Family photos record our life as a family. I have kept all of the clothes I sewed for the girls. They may never use them, but I could never discard proof that I once actually knew how to sew.

Simplicity is a highly desired state, an ongoing effort, a relief when it finally arrives. Simplicity allows me to keep the best, let go of the rest, and smile my way through the dresser drawers, piles, and trunks of memories.

Love,

Dee Dee

Like many people today, I still strive for a simpler life. Remembering the lessons of simplicity is somehow easier than claiming the victory of actually living a simple life. Life is infinitely more complicated than it was when my housing point of reference was simply "Old House" or "New."

THE MANSION ON THE PRAIRIE

Dear Mom,

When I tell people I grew up without indoor plumbing, no one believes me. I'm way too young, they think. I know better. The "Old House" was a small 600-square-foot, three-room house plus a porch. The living room held the antique cedar chest, old furniture, the oil furnace, and the TV. Curtains graced the double hung windows, adding coziness to the living room where I got my first gun and holster set, my first plastic bowling balls and pins, and where I watched the bubble lights glisten and glow on the Christmas tree.

The Old House did not have indoor plumbing. The only way we had water was by getting a bucket of it from the outdoor pump. We took baths once a week in a metal tub, and of course, used the outhouse for the bathroom. The outhouse gave us more than one use for Reader's Digest *and the Sears Roebuck catalog. It was really an early form of recycling.*

The kitchen in the Old House featured the metal table that held my first six birthday cakes. Birthday cakes were always angel food with pink Beat & Eat frosting, whipped to perfection. The old Hot Point fridge and freezer, cook stove and a tall corner cupboard filled in the rest of the room. An enamel bucket held water and a dipper for drinking.

In 1962, we built and moved into the "New House," another simple definition that has stuck. I was six when we built the New House. I remember the day that dad's brother, Uncle Clarence, started digging the basement. That hole in the ground that became the basement seemed so huge. Uncle Clarence laid the cement bricks with mortar, scraping away the excess by hand. Kermit Peterson and Guff Moen were the construction workers helping Clarence. They put up the two-foot by four-foot boards, framing in the house. I remember when we walked on the floor to outline the room layouts. I thought my 10-foot by 10-foot room was so huge. I told myself that the bed would only take up this little corner, the dresser that little corner, and the whole rest of the room was destined to be my new indoor playground!

The New House was a mansion compared to the Old House, and yet the floor was only 28-foot by 40-foot. The kitchen had new wood cabinets, a copper-colored Kenmore stove and oven, white refrigerator, and the same old table and chairs from the Old House. The living room had new furniture, a three-sectioned couch, old chairs from the Old House, and new end tables. The bathroom was immense, with a built-in vanity, sink with a cupboard around it, medicine cabinet, and a white toilet and white bathtub. The bedrooms held a combination of new furniture and Grandma and Grandpa's bedroom furniture, including the big, round mirror. It would be a wonderful antique today.

The walls were white, blue, and pink. I actually had pink paint on my bedroom walls. That's the only time in my life I've had pink walls. We had crucifixes in all of the rooms, complete with braided palms from Palm Sunday services of the previous year.

The color of the house was the best, aqua blue that seemed to *match the prairie skies. White trim matched the rocks we painted white and used to line the driveway to separate gravel from grass.*

We had a "double car" garage that seemed huge to a child. It wasn't. I wonder how we ever parked anything in it.

It's funny how size changes as we age. What seemed huge was small by today's standards. Overall, the best part of the New House was that water ran out of things called faucets, into containers called sinks and bathtubs. Now that was huge, Mom. That feature alone made the New House on the prairie seem like the Mansion.

Love,

Dee Dee

After living in such a small house, the New House was a mansion indeed. Indoor plumbing came in 1962 and heralded progress at full speed. And yet it is true: we had television before we had indoor plumbing.

THE WORLD VIA TV AND A MOVIE

Dear Mom,

Television brought us visual proof of great and tragic events. I was seven when the assassin killed President John Kennedy. We watched, sad and teary, as black horses drew his coffin down Pennsylvania Avenue in D.C. The riderless horse seemed especially sad, as did the salute from JFK Junior. We witnessed Jack Ruby kill Lee Harvey Oswald. We watched rockets launch, and we stayed glued to the TV as Apollo 11 struggled back to earth. Riots played out in front of us, as did the Vietnam War images.

The television broadcasting the world into the heart of our living rooms affected my generation. We wanted to join the revolution, make a difference, or create justice in the world. I hated the pictures of racial injustice, especially in my all-white world of northeastern South Dakota. I hated the Vietnam War, mostly because Dad didn't think we belonged there. He was a highly decorated WWII vet, and I felt he understood what I had yet to learn.

I wanted to be a hippie, Mom, but it was so hard in Roslyn, and impossible on the farm. Rick thought rock and roll was bad, and since he controlled the radio, I was forced to listen to Buck Owens, Hank Williams, Sr., Ernest Tubb, and Hank Snow. I could sing the words to "Your Cheatin' Heart," "I've Got a Tiger by the Tail," and "The Tennessee Waltz."

In fact, Mom, it wasn't until most of the songs of the 60s became known as Golden Oldies that I heard them for the first time. Can you believe that? No wonder I was so naive! It changed after we moved off the farm and I was around "town kids" with whom I attended dances and listened to car radios.

Television brought us the life of JFK, and the movie screen brought his WWII heroism. The JFK era led us to the only movie we ever went to see as a family. "PT109" played in Webster, and we went to see Kennedy, the hero, in the beautiful Pacific Ocean, the same blue water your husband saw in the same war. I wonder how you felt, seeing the place where your husband's heroism earned three Bronze Stars and the Purple Heart.

Love,

Dee Dee

As Mom and Dad outfitted our house with modern conveniences, the prairie weather continued its seasons. Cold days and mounds of snow did not keep us indoors. As children, we were too active to get cold. Maybe the woolen hats, mittens, hooded parkas and snow pants kept us warm. On the other hand, maybe it was our knowing that Mom's hot chocolate waited for us after we built yet another snow fort or snow tunnel.

Snow Days and Snow Forts

Dear Mom,

It snowed here today in Cheyenne, where people get excited at even a few inches. They have no idea what real snow on the prairie is like and how great an old-fashioned blizzard can be.

Snow was a way of redefining the playground. On the farm, instead of playing in the trees, we played in the snow. We made snow forts by cutting blocks of the hard, wind-blown snow banks. We stacked the blocks into a small building, complete with a door and a window. Then we poured water over the blocks to create an ice fort that would last until spring thaw.

We dug snow tunnels into the snow banks, and we had great snowball fights. Dad would pull us on the round metal saucer sled that attached to the back of the pickup by a long rope. He would pull us on the snow-covered alfalfa field, swinging us and teaching us the thrill of holding on for a great ride. No helmets, of course, Mom. It was the mid-60s. I wonder how we ever stayed warm.

At school we played "duck-duck, goose-goose," making circular patterns in the snow. Because we never lacked snow, we still played on the playground equipment, including the huge slide, especially if you were naïve enough to take a dare and lick the surface. Think of the tongue tissue that stuck to the metal as my blood gushed. Naïve me, another victim of a playground dare.

Then there was my first blizzard. I woke up on my own, wondering why you hadn't gotten me out of bed at the usual time for school. I walked into the kitchen, surprised to see you and Dad sitting there. Normally he would be outside tending to the cattle and doing chores.

I looked puzzled as you explained a blizzard meant that there was no school. I must have looked perplexed, because Dad said that this probably was my first real blizzard. He told me to look out the window. I did, and saw that the normal view of the barn, the trees, the grass, and the cattle disappeared into the white sheet. The blowing snow of a blizzard is an anomaly with zero visibility. You didn't walk into it unless you had a rope tied to you, attached to the building. You could absolutely get lost in that kind of storm, and death would come quickly.

I had heard some of Laura Ingalls Wilder's blizzard stories, of how Pa and Ma Ingalls and the family survived those vicious winter storms on that same prairie. We were that "Little House on the Prairie," as the storm raged for three days. It only meant three days of no school and more snow forts and tunnels. Not a bad deal for a kid on the prairie!

Love,

Dee Dee

Red cheeks, hot chocolate, the sense of accomplishment from building a snow fort that would last until spring thaw. Just another perfect winter day on the prairie! Another aspect of being raised on the prairie is that some of us flatlanders enjoy mountain vistas, but not the hairpin turns while driving.

FLATLANDER

Dear Mom,

How different our worlds have been, Mom. Your world was limited to travel in five states. The boundaries of your travel experience were Minneapolis to the east, Helena to the west, with the Dakotas and Sioux City in between. You were always home. Going out meant that you were with all of us kids, visiting relatives, or attending family reunions in Starbuck, Minnesota.

I still remember the only time you left us for a trip. You went to Helena, Montana, to visit Aunt Gertrude and other relatives for about a week. You left us on the farm with Dad. Thank God he knew how to cook. I heard the story about your fear of the mountains. You hated that the road was on the edge of the mountains, and when you peered into the depth down the mountain, your stomach tightened. Did you say you would never travel there again?

Maybe you are the reason I'm not a mountain person. I love to look at them, and I have enjoyed them, but my mountain friends call me a flatlander for a reason. I don't even have a fear of heights. I just don't like looking down the mountain from the back seat of a car. I don't like skiing, and when I snowmobile, I watch others climb the mountains from my sled safely positioned in the middle of the meadow. I don't have knees for mountain hiking, and going downhill on skis is in my category of "one-timers." Now put me on cross-country skis on the prairie, and I'm set for a great day!

I have traveled much more than you did, Mom. I've enjoyed ocean sunrises and sunsets that you never saw. I have enjoyed islands, forests, and Asian countries, and my goal is to get to Europe. My world has been much bigger than yours, Mom. However, here is my secret—I still haven't been to Helena, Montana!

Love,

Dee Dee

Chapter Six

Wealth
Is Real
Prairie Food

Hospitality in the prairie country is not limited.
Even if your enemy passes away,
you must feed him before you shoot him.

O. Henry

Hospitality on the prairie binds our small communities together. Our hospitable traditions mean that no person is a stranger. When a neighbor is ill or dies, you bring the best food and favorite recipe from your kitchen as an act of compassion. We celebrate births, carnivals, or church socials in the same air of frivolity and food.

Did you know that the delicious food on your table travels an average of 2,000 miles to get to you? That simple fact of today's modern world makes me relish the gold nuggets of local recipes that use local foods. It is not just that the local tasty treats come from the region in which we live; they are part of the history of this people's hearts and souls, let alone tummies and taste buds.

No Cooking Like Mom's

Dear Mom,

Rich, thick German chocolate frosting totally made from scratch. Pineapple bars with thin, sweet dough, a sugary pineapple filling, topped with powdered-sugar icing. Melt-in-your-mouth chocolate brownies with always-perfect homemade frosting. Are you drooling yet, Mom?

I get hungry just thinking about the delicious varieties and tastes of your food. You just had a way about you, Mom. The dough in anything you made was from scratch and perfectly thin, sweet, and delicious. The frostings were thick, smooth, and so easy to swallow. I didn't know frosting came in a can.

I love to make chocolate cake from scratch, with sour milk and homemade chocolate frosting. But my family does something very insulting with it. They put a piece of cake in a glass and cover it with milk. It's so dishonoring to a work of art like homemade cake. I feel a connection to you, the great baker and cook, every time I create something from nothing. I make the chocolate cake with homemade frosting only for special occasions because that's the only time I can handle the disrespect shown by eating it in a glass of milk.

My family thinks I'm crazy for that. Maybe I am. I just believe that artwork, in any form, is worthy and should be honored, not drowned in milk! Jessie honored me last night, Mom. She called Kelsey from college and had one primary message for her: don't take Mom's cooking for granted. She misses it and wants Kelsey to appreciate the good food she gets every day.

Yes, that was honoring. That makes me want to cook for them. Putting the cake in the glass of milk makes me want to put them on a no-chocolate diet for the rest of my life with them!

Love,

Dee Dee

Women like my mother took pride in what they grew, produced, and baked. Their best desserts, salads and fried chicken were proudly shared with others. Family members loved Mom's baked beans and potato salad, and school bake sales meant we proudly offered Mom's mouthwatering homemade brownies, topped with miniature marshmallows, drizzled with chocolate icing.

Every spring, when the prairie produced a new crop of rhubarb, Mom would delight us with the first-of-the-season Rhubarb Torte, complete with perfect meringue. I hope you enjoy my mother's delicious recipe for my favorite dessert, the one for which she received accolades.

RHUBARB TORTE

Crust:
1-cup flour
1/2 cup butter
2 T sugar
1/8 tsp. salt

Blend and pat into 9" square pan. Bake 22 - 30 minutes at 350 degrees.

Filling:
3 egg yolks
2 T flour
1 cup sugar
2 1/4 cups cut rhubarb
1/3 cup sour cream

Beat egg yolks well. Mix sugar, cream, egg yolks and flour, mix with rhubarb, pour into pan. Cook until thick. Pour hot onto hot crust. Top with meringue.

Meringue:
3 egg whites
1/4 tsp. cream of tartar
Pinch of salt
1/2 cup sugar

Beat egg whites until frothy; add salt, cream of tartar. Gradually add sugar. Beat until meringue forms stiff peaks and the sugar dissolves. Bake 20 - 25 minutes, 350 degrees, or until meringue is brown and dry.

HOMEMADE ICE CREAM

Dear Mom,

One of my favorite treats is making homemade ice cream in the winter. When I ask friends over for homemade ice cream, they say they love it, but they've never made it in the wintertime. When else would you make it? We only made homemade ice cream when it was cold outside.

On the farm, we had a wooden ice cream bucket that held the ice, freshly chopped from the cattle tank; the container that held the real cream, fresh from the cream separator in the barn, with farm-fresh eggs and vanilla; and a handle that we cranked forever. It was real ice cream, soft, and delicious.

But why only in winter? Because that's when we had ice. You and Dad grew up without electricity, and therefore, no freezer. You got your ice from the cattle tank. However, even when we had a freezer, we still got our ice by chopping it from the cattle tank. "We," of course, were Rick and Dad. I didn't chop. I don't think I even turned the handle. I just enjoyed the ice cream.

Several years after you died, we had Christmas at Gayle's house. Rick's part of the day was to bring everything to make homemade ice cream. "EVERYTHING," I said, when we discussed it on the telephone. I was bringing the ice cream maker and other food. He was bringing all the ingredients and everything else needed to make the delicious treat.

Well, my brother did pretty well, except he forgot ice. Not to worry! He went down to the slough and chopped ice. Once again, we had homemade ice cream, made possible by winter in South Dakota. What a delicious wintertime treat. Thanks for that memory, Mom!

Love,

Dee Dee

When winter thawed, warmer weather and clear skies always meant gardening. Seed catalogs in hand, Mom would plan and order. Then she prepared the soil, planted the seeds or plants, and harvested in the fall. We children would occasionally help, sometimes weeding and picking, but usually, simply enjoying.

Summer meals meant fresh green beans, lettuce, radishes, cucumbers, potatoes, onions, corn, carrots, and the very best: peas. We would sneak into the garden and enjoy peas, plucked fresh from pods. Mom always wanted enough for a meal; we thought sneaking into the garden counted toward that meal.

CHOKECHERRIES: PRIZE OF THE PRAIRIE

Dear Mom,

Our friends in Casper gave us with one of the best Christmas presents this year. It was a basket full of homemade jellies and jams: chokecherry, raspberry, blueberry, and strawberry. The prize of the prairie is homemade chokecherry jelly, Mom. It doesn't get any better.

You were the master of homemade chokecherry jelly. We picked berries by the buckets and proudly handed them to you. You did the rest: washed them carefully, boiled them down, made the jelly, and served it proudly. The best part was the mistake. Whenever jelly didn't thicken properly, we used it as syrup over pancakes. Wow! What a treat that was.

Picking chokecherries with Rick was not a treat on hot days in the middle of July or early August when the berries were ripe. In South Dakota's prairie, that meant days of 90 degrees and high humidity.

Pete Waletich, our neighbor from Yugoslavia, asked Rick to pick chokecherries, as he used them for making wine. Pete made a lot of wine, didn't he? It's something I'm sure he learned in what he always said was "the old country."

Rick and I picked chokecherries one humid day for Pete. I had a small bucket, and Rick had what must have been a five-gallon pail full of berries. Since I was so much smaller, Pete paid me the same he paid Rick. Rick still hasn't let me forget that one.

Rick also started making chokecherry wine, having learned how from one of the best. He used large glass bottles with balloons on the top that would expand as the wine processed. One night after we were all asleep, there was an explosion in the house that sounded like dynamite. We found Rick in bed with millions of glass shards all around him and wine sprayed over every inch of the room. One of the glass containers had exploded. Luckily, Rick wasn't hurt. The room was a disaster, though. I wonder if he made any more wine after that.

Chokecherries were one of the very best parts of growing up on the farm, Mom. The gift from our friends brought back a flavor full of memories

Love,

Dee Dee

The harvest from Mom's garden meant shelves full of jars, and a freezer and cellar full of food for the winter. Mom canned jars of all sizes with green beans, beet pickles, dill pickles, sweet pickles, cherries, apples and preserves, including plum, chokecherry jelly and apple butter. The freezer was full of corn and pies, made only from fresh apples from Grandma's orchards, and the cellar held potatoes, squash, and onions.

Farmers today would call our process organic gardening. I'm sure it was done under the hot sun, with mosquitoes making the day miserable. What I remember most is the incredible taste of fresh produce, grown in black dirt, cut or picked fresh, washed, cooked and served, day in, day out. It doesn't get any better.

If we didn't grow our food or raise it, we hunted or fished for it. The glacial lakes where I grew up were abundant sources of migrating waterfowl and pan fish. While I didn't hunt, I loved to fish for perch, blue gills or bullheads. Fish was, after all, a menu item we could count on at least one day of every week.

FISH ON FRIDAYS

Dear Mom,

Fish on Fridays was the rule. We knew it. Even though we lived on a Hereford cattle farm, we upheld the rule and ate fish on Fridays.

Catholics had many rules: cover heads in church, do not turn around and speak to a neighbor, follow the sequence of prayers and respond accordingly, sing when appropriate. We had to learn the Catholic rules and doctrines in catechism classes, and we had to listen to the nuns.

It was the years before Vatican II that I remember the most. Priests said masses in Latin until I was seven. I wonder how many church services I went to where I really did not understand anything. I think Latin is beautiful, and I still recall parts of the service, especially the "Mea culpa, mea culpa, mea maxima culpa." However, Latin made it all too easy to disconnect from the meaning. I didn't get it, even though I tried.

I also tried to be good in catechism. I remember lifelong lessons learned as the nuns taught us the Ten Commandments in third grade. When the sister got to the part about adultery, our quizzical looks reflected our confusion. Her red face and stammer revealed that it had to do with touching ourselves.

Well, I took everything quite literally when I was in third grade. Dutifully, I confessed the sin of adultery in my next confession with Father Nemmers. In his sermon the next Sunday, Father Nemmers talked about how we had some work to do in Catholic education because little kids cannot commit adultery. Boy, was I confused as I touched myself when I scratched, washed, brushed my teeth, and combed my hair. What was I supposed to think? Had I or hadn't I committed adultery? How was a third-grader to know?

Fish on Fridays was a simple rule. Others were more complicated. At least once we got to the point of speaking English in the service I had a better chance of understanding—adultery or not!

Love ya,

Dee Dee

SECTION FOUR

Priceless Lessons

Every trial endured and weathered
in the right spirit
makes a soul nobler and stronger
than it was before.

James Buckham

CHAPTER SEVEN

Generational Wisdom

Learn wisdom from the ways of the seedling.
A seedling which is never hardened off
through stressful situations
will never become a strong productive plant.

Stephen Sigmund

Adlai Stevenson once said that the absurdity of one generation becomes the wisdom of another. My mother's generation was shaped by the Depression and led her to be thrifty, talented with her hands, and patient in her creations. My generation was more prosperous and demanding, having been introduced to the immediate satisfaction delivered by fast food and the ease of department store shopping. As the world got faster and more complicated, my generation's responses included agitation and stress from the lack of patience.

As we mature, we may find wisdom in some of our parents' ways through our journey of memories. Today I value the simplicity and thriftiness of my mother. She had a great respect for people and the land, wasting nothing. I find that lesson to be priceless.

DO IT WELL

Dear Mom,

This is the big moment; Jessie is going to college. She went to the local community college this fall, the same fall she turned 19. Now, she's preparing to leave us and attend South Dakota State University in Brookings, a school that's 11 hours away and my alma mater.

I wonder how you felt when I left for college. Were you scared for me? You never showed fear. I sensed more relief. I had actually gotten through high school and was off to college. Besides, it was only two hours from home. You never went to college, but you always supported me, plain and simple.

What you taught me wasn't about competition against somebody else. Your wisdom to my generation was to do the best I could, competing with myself. You told me repeatedly, "If you're going to bother to do something, do it well." This seems a simple standard, yet a tough one.

That standard meant I had to have the topstitching perfect on clothes. It meant giving every school paper my best shot. It meant practicing percussion for hours on end.

Now I think about my own daughter going off to college, the lessons I learned from you, and the lessons I passed on to her. I wonder if Jessie will give things her best shot. With you looking down as her guardian angel, Mom, I am sure she will.

Love,

Dee Dee

Wisdom born of our parents' and grandparents' experiences provides our heartfelt values. Values are the picture frame that holds the canvas of our beliefs and textures of life. My mother's generation seemed a resilient group, united for the war effort, respectful of finances, able to "get by" and "make do" with what they had. My family's old junker represented that straightforward value.

OLD BROWN FORD

Dear Mom,

Jessie drives, and Kelsey wants to drive. They both want new cars. They think it is not fair to have old junkers like the car we drove: the great old brown 1959 Ford.

It never occurred to me that we couldn't afford a new car.

Dad always said that we would get one, although it never happened. I wish I had that Ford today because it would be a classic, but in the 60s, it was just an old car.

Seat belts weren't an issue in the 60s. We simply did not have any, so wearing them was not an option. We didn't talk about safety. I guess in rural South Dakota in the 60s, safety wasn't much of an issue either.

I remember how embarrassed you were the day a middle-aged "city" guy stopped by the farm to inquire about the old Ford. It sat next to the house, and the man thought he could use our old junker for spare parts. There was a stern quality in your voice as you said, "No," that was our car, the one we drove when we went somewhere.

I remember visiting cousins who teased me about that car. Kids can be cruel without trying very hard. They had nice cars, and they just couldn't understand why we didn't.

It was an old junker, but it was ours. I think humble beginnings are good, and I am grateful for mine, Mom. It taught me what really matters. What better lesson can you get from growing up?

Love,

Dee Dee

How can a child really know the wisdom of the parent until you can view life as a parent yourself? Until I embody or give meaning to my mother's listening to me practice my drumming incessantly, I would not understand the value of tolerance. Unless I helped her plant the garden, harvest the food and prepare a meal, would I know its worth? Could I assign merit to any experience as a child without the adult to cheer me on, model the behaviors, and support the commitments I made? Perhaps then, the real value is the *presence* of the mother for the child, even silent in the background, as a reminder of who you are and what you are worth as a human being.

THE RED DRUMSTICKS

Dear Mom,

In 1990, your granddaughter and three of her friends decided to give me a concert after having played their musical instruments for less than one month. It was a delightful cacophony of sound. The players were energetic, loving entertainers who were launching their musical careers on a piano, a flute, and a clarinet.

Twenty-five years earlier, in 1965, your third-grade daughter began her musical career by paying $2 for a pair of bright red drumsticks. Remember, Mom? My teacher was Mr. Charles Urbin, a former member of the Berlin symphony who had found his way across the world to teach music in Roslyn, South Dakota, or so I was told. He seemed old, and I assumed he was at least 80 at the time.

I drummed from third grade through my sophomore year of college. I don't know if I was good, but I know I loved it and practiced a lot.

My practicing must have driven you crazy. I wonder how many drummers were forced to go outside and practice on boards or barn doors because they were noisy. How did you ever survive the Christmas vacation when my teacher let me take the trap set home, cymbals and all? It must have been one huge headache for you. The sound bounced off those cement block walls right up the staircase to where you were trying to watch your soaps.

I will always love you for being proud of me. Every little girl needs one cheerleader to encourage her. I remember how proud you were, Mom, when I brought home a Superior Plus on my first solo in 8th grade. You were proud at concerts when I performed a solo or our jazz band played a great version of Glenn Miller's "In the Mood." Perhaps it was your pride that helped you tolerate my unceasing practice, twirling sticks, and practice sessions. I understand why you were thrilled when I won a rubber practice pad!

Thanks for all the support you gave my musical career, Mom. You put up with uncountable hours of noise that I proudly called music. You taught me how to enjoy my own daughters' musical careers with a smile and no earplugs.

Love,

Dee Dee

No daughter could appreciate a mother being so supportive in her education more than I did. It was her small—yet huge—way of showing her love. For a child, Valentine's Day was one day when I could express mine: "Roses are red, violets are blue, someone in third grade really loves you!"

HAPPY VALENTINE'S DAY!

Dear Mom,

Kim gave Kelsey a dozen red roses for Valentine's Day. He gave me a dozen yellow roses, and he sent Jessie roses at college. He's the flower-giving man this year.

Actually, Mom, Kim does that every year. It's a lovely tradition, and it reminds me of childhood Valentine traditions, and how special this day has always been.

In grade school, we wrote on small, decorative valentines for classmates for our annual party. How embarrassing it was to write "Love, Dee Ann" on cards that seemed mushy. Then again, deep down inside I liked it because the phrase gave me a taste of the future relationships we would someday have. Valentine's Day meant that we sent cards from Jessie and Kelsey to all three great-grandmothers and four grandparents. It was a holiday where it was safe to express your love for someone, with or without flowers. Hallmark provided greetings that were perfect for those special people.

I remember walking into the Hallmark store in Pierre a few weeks before Valentine's Day, 1991. It was my first Valentine's Day without you; and the first one for my daughters not to send you a card; the first year where I couldn't send a card to "Mom and Dad." I had to look for a card that read "Dad," but all I could see was the Hallmark "Mom" on the card rack in front of me. All Mom cards printed in deep reds with hearts and flowers made me cry. I felt robbed of sending you a Valentine's card and expressing my feelings. I had given you one nearly every Valentine's Day of my entire life, and now, I faced the reality of no more cards for my mom. No more, ever.

How many times I wished I'd said "I love you," Mom, on

every single phone call, in every letter, every time I saw you, and each time I left you. I wish I had been able to say, "I love you" more than just on Valentine's Day. So let me say it now.

I love the one who wore bright red lipstick, polyester pants, made crafts with her granddaughters, and baked the best cookies and desserts in the world. I love the traditions you created for us, and the fact that you were simply always there.

I love you, Mom.

Happy Valentine's Day!

Love,

Dee Dee

CHAPTER EIGHT

Passing The Wisdom Forward

Wisdom is knowledge, rightly applied.

Unknown

Yes, Mom's world of my childhood seemed less complicated on the farm because our world was smaller, by geography as well as education. On the other hand, now our children hurry through their day to meet the globalization they face in adulthood. Are my daughters prepared? Are my cherished traditions enough to sustain their faith as they rush to their future? Will my daughters feel as naive as I felt?

JESSIE

Dear Mom,

I really had no clue about being pregnant the first time. I recall the hot humid day in July when you had my new baby sister, Gayle, in 1959. I couldn't visit you in the hospital, but I talked to you through the window of your hospital room. I remember asking you for a stick of chewing gum. I was only three.

Then I saw you pregnant in 1966, and that was my extent of knowledge of pregnancy and babies. I babysat as a kid, and I may have learned a little about babies in home economics class. Even so, I really had no clue what I was getting into when I had Jessica.

First, there was the name. The only name Kim and I could agree on was Jessie, or Jesse if a boy. Boy or girl, the name was Jessie. Then there was the morning sickness, five months of throwing up.

All of the sudden, there she was. Jessica Elizabeth Raap was born at 11:44 a.m. on October 1, 1980. Kim was concerned over such a long name. After all, Jessie has half the alphabet in her name. I understood that a man with three syllables for the entire name—Kim Vern Raap—would probably have an understandable concern. Moreover, our daughter was going to have Elizabeth in her name. That was certain.

I remember your story of how I was born with a mop of black hair. You said I wore a ponytail at four months. Well, I married a blonde-haired person, and when I produced a baby with black hair, I wasn't surprised, but Kim was shocked.

Your granddaughter, Jessica Elizabeth Raap, is the oldest daughter, of the oldest daughter, of the oldest daughter, of the oldest daughter. In addition, we all have Elizabeth in our names. Jessica Elizabeth Raap. My confirmation name was Elizabeth. You were born Elizabeth Kathryn Weyer. Your mother was born Elizabeth Theresa Tanata. It is a tradition that we maintain—half the alphabet or not. I know that the name is important for our mother line, and what a major decision it was in my life! I really had no clue, did I, Mom?

Love,

Dee Dee

Whether we feel naive or wise as we journey through life, what's most important is that we learn from our experience. Our learning is guided by the values we brought with us from childhood, values we feel deeply. A good example is my desire to add Elizabeth to Jessica's name. I cannot logically explain why we named a first-born daughter of each mother in my family Elizabeth. The emotional reason is that it defines the courage of heart in my family. It is the *feelings of* mother, home, security, and caring that we hold dear.

You Can Go Home Again

Dear Mom,

Relocating is one of the most difficult things I've done. Kim and I moved from Sioux Falls, a community of more than 100,000 people, to Roy Lake, near Lake City, South Dakota, when Jessie was two. I thought I would die living in a state park two miles from Lake City, a town of 44 people. I was a full-time mom for the first time, in a place with no prospect of a job. My dream of being with Jessie was real, and it scared me to death. As they say, you should watch out what you pray for!

Tom Wolfe said you can't go home again. Maybe Roy Lake was just far enough away from Roslyn that it wasn't actually home. After all, it was only 20 miles away. I hated moving there, and every day when Kim got home from work at 4:30, I was walking off my frustration at 4:32. I walked two miles as fast as I could, day after day. After many days of walking, I finally surrendered my will to God on the beach, saying there must be a reason for my living here.

In retrospect, much of the reason was growing closer to you and Dad. Dad was great. He would drive up to see me. One day he walked into the garage and I said, "Thank God you're here. I was just getting ready to move back to Sioux Falls." We made coffee and talked. A few weeks later, the same thing happened again, and his response was, "Again?" His listening, knowing, and being there for me was great.

The best part of living at Roy Lake was having Kelsey. After Jessie, I figured I knew what to expect, but that was the wrong conclusion. I was sick again, but in a different way. After six months, I felt as normal as a six-month pregnant woman feels. My doctor was an old family friend. I drove to Watertown, which was 80 miles away, for my checkups. Watertown was where we would deliver Kelsey.

My labor with Jessie was only six hours. Kelsey was due on Monday, and through his daughter-in-law, my doctor learned that I had begun having inconsistent contractions over the weekend. On Monday morning, my doctor called and asked what I was doing. I said I was just hanging around, having a few contractions. My doctor laughed and said, "Get on the bus, babe!" So we went to Watertown, stayed at Gennie and Roger's, and got up in the middle of the night to have Kelsey.

It was scary Mom, because it was so different from having Jessie. I had incredible back pain. Turns out she had flipped just days before delivery, and was coming out face down. Plus, she was much bigger than Jessie, so I tore. But it was worth it. Kelsey was one incredible special gift; she was born at 6:06 a.m., June 12, 1984. Now it was four of us living together on the prairie of South Dakota. Who said you can't go home again?

Love,

Dee Dee

In my journey through memories after losing Mom, I looked closely at my mothering adventures. What is laughable are some of my beliefs about mothering! Hindsight is always better, right?

KELSEY

Dear Mom,

The fact that Rick was a boy and I was a girl made it logical to me that he and I would be different. I applied the same logic to having two girls. They would be similar, since they were both girls, right? How wrong I was!

Kelsey was born with an attitude—a great, strong-willed mindset—but an attitude nonetheless. Does the second child have the advantage of observation that the first child lacks? Kelsey assessed any situation based upon her needs and the consequences faced by Jessie, and she knew how to best circumvent and navigate to her advantage. In other words, she figured us out before we figured her out.

Kelsey's attitude today is a wonderful mixture of intelligence, caring and faith. You would be proud, Mom. She taught sixth grade Sunday school this year with another sophomore, and she brought her faith with her.

Today's world is confusing for kids, Mom. There are millions of mixed messages from society, families, schools, and the kid's peers. Kelsey has an inner compass guiding her. Thank God for that.

Love,

Dee Dee

I like being at the age of watching my children mature into their good judgment. I appreciate the phone calls from college to discuss academic pressures, boyfriends, and recipes. Any mom enjoys seeing the next generation make responsible choices. It helps us feel like we are contributing!

But, I can't say that was always the case!

Used Mom

Dear Mom,

I once gave a speech titled "Used Mom." I compared myself as a mom to a used car—dented, scratched, and chips of paint missing here and there. Once upon a time, I was brand new, clean, and polished. Then I had kids.

Mom, you once got angry for something I had done. You looked at me, shook a finger, and said, "Someday, your kids are going to do to you EXACTLY what you've done to me." I was perplexed. How could they? First, I wasn't planning to have children. Secondly, if I did, mine would be angelic.

Angelic is not the word to describe the gift God gives you in two teenage daughters. Two teenage daughters can run you ragged and keep you concerned and barely coherent. You very much resemble an old, used car. Just ask my daughters.

At times, Jessie and Kelsey say they don't understand me. I think I am speaking plain, simple English, but I must have picked up a foreign language along the way and used it when addressing my daughters. Or else I was in a stress-induced state that led to incoherent mumbling. Why else would they totally ignore me?

There is an easy answer to that one. Tradition! In the same tradition that I ignored you, they ignore me. Only they weren't supposed to! I was a much more intelligent, informed mother than you were, Mom. I read the books! I attended the classes! I had great friends who helped me through the motherhood maze! Things were going to be different for my kids than when I was a teenager. But you guessed it. You already knew it when I was a teen. You knew I would have daughters who say the same things, show up late, be a mess, and seem indifferent. You knew that all of the trouble and gray hair I gave you would be my inheritance as well.

Why else would you have warned me? Why would I now issue the same warning to my daughters? Yes, I, too, have pointed a finger and said, "Someday, your children are going to do the EXACT same thing you have done to me." I know you were just grinning from your seat in heaven when you heard me. Are you still smiling, Mom?

Love,

Dee Dee

I once read a quote by Peter DeVries that sums up what happens when we become parents: "Who of us is mature enough for offspring before the offspring themselves arrive? The value in marriage is not that adults produce children, but that children produce adults." So instead of children blaming parents for what they become, we can now lay the blame on our children. At least I've told my daughters so.

PARENTAL LESSONS LEARNED

Dear Mom,

One lesson I've learned is that there is no more humbling profession than that of a parent. God fully intended to keep us humble when He gave us children. He gives tips on how to keep parents humble to every baby about to be born. In addition, the children He gives us take that job seriously.

I remember how your face fell when we embarrassed you through our play and actions. It happened when we pointed out you were playing cards with a deck of 51. It happened when we suggested you were being "stingy" by giving us frozen, year-old raspberries instead of the ones you'd just picked from your garden. It happened when I told my first grade teacher that Dad got the bumps on his head from you hitting him with the rolling pin. Well, Mom, what goes around comes around. One beautiful, summer Sunday in Pierre, one of the most embarrassing moments of my life occurred.

We were going to church, one of your basic Lutheran churches in South Dakota. Both girls looked great in their sundresses, white anklets, clean shoes and brushed, shiny hair held back with colorful plastic barrettes. I looked at them and thought how great they looked, and what a great mom I was for making sure they looked so nice. Life was going well.

In church, Kelsey, who was three, stood on the pew so she could see. While the minister was reading the gospel, and everyone was quietly listening, Kelsey pulled her sundress up around her neck and proudly, rather defiantly, proclaimed, "I don't got NO panties on!" And she didn't have a stitch on that little butt! I have never fully recovered, but she does wear panties to church. And, I remain one of God's humbled parents.

In all humility,

Dee Dee

SECTION FIVE

Seasons Of The Prairie

Treat the earth well: it was not given to you by your parents,
it was loaned to you by your children.
We do not inherit the Earth from our Ancestors;
we borrow it from our Children.

Ancient Proverb

CHAPTER NINE

The Prairie

So if you think that plastic pink flamingos
are a thing of the past,
I'm here to tell you it isn't so.
There will always be someone out there
whose idea of beauty is a pink plastic bird
standing among their red petunias.[4]

I sit in a Mexican restaurant at the Iberostar Resort in Cozumel and watch and listen to pink flamingos. Real ones chase each other, circling ponds, screeching loudly in a morning ritual.

It's impossible for me not to think about my mother's pink flamingos, plastic bodies with long necks, held up by three-foot, skinny metal poles. They stood in front of pink and white petunia beds, adding color to our front yard on the South Dakota prairie.

I always wondered why they were there. I had never seen a pink flamingo on the prairie. Ducks with green heads, geese with white and black feathers, black crows that appeared blue? Yes, but never pink flamingos!

I am sure Mom had never seen a real one either, having never traveled farther south than Sioux City, Iowa. So why the pink flamingos? Mom wanted to grace her harsh prairie environment with beauty, and perhaps a bit of "culture." For that same reason, she painted field rocks white and placed them on the edge of the grass to create a border for our yard. She planted moss roses in the antique green enamel tub, and had lilacs and peonies that the free-roaming sheep loved and devoured. Mom's home on the prairie deserved the charm and beauty seen in magazines, and she fulfilled that need every spring.

Married to a farmer, Mom took on the domestic chores of raising four children on the same prairie my great-grandmother homesteaded in 1882. More than one hundred years later, South Dakota can be still a harsh place—hot, humid summers, cold winters, and strong winds.

THE HOMESTEAD

Dear Mom,

I didn't know until just a few years ago that my great-grandmother homesteaded the land where Dad lived as a child. Then you grew up on that farm. When I first took Kim there, I realized the beauty of the area. Kim was in awe of the hills, the sloughs, the trees, and all the wildlife. Deer, ducks, and geese call it home.

My great-grandmother came from Wisconsin, a widow with two small children. She was my dad's grandmother, so no relation of yours. I think of her often as I wonder what life was like for her on that property. Did she think it was beautiful the first time she saw it, like Kim? Or did she come to appreciate its beauty later in life, as I did? What was it like in 1882 to live with two small children on the prairie? How did she survive and keep her sanity?

Some days on the farm were so boring, Mom. The word routine described many days of hot, dry summers, haying, chasing cattle, and mowing lawns. To a young girl, it was the same boring routine, day in, and day out, not very exciting, no fun.

These days I crave routine. I want to be bored, just for a while. Life seems so unpredictable and full of twists and turns. We talk of moving, new careers, and while it sounds good, part of me just doesn't want to change again. I have lived in 10 different houses since I married Kim. With 10 moves behind me, is it any wonder why I crave simplicity?

How much "stuff" did my great-grandmother move with her when she came to homestead in South Dakota? What decisions did she make in one day? I speculate if she found routine boring or comforting.

The farm is still there. The buildings are not used, but the house is still standing. I wish the big, old, red barn could be repaired because they don't build them like that any more. The chicken coop still stands where Grandma and I fed the chickens and geese. I relish the smell of the farm, the view of the sloughs, and what was a very long walk from the barn to the house for a little person with short legs.

Distances were so relative back then. Everything seemed so far, and we didn't travel anywhere often. Yet, the road to that farm held special meaning for me then, as it does to this day. Nearly every time we visited Dad, we drove him to the farm to look at the old buildings, the old tree claim, and the rented fields that now grow corn. Having the farm in the family 118 years after my great-grandmother made it her home is like a comfortable warm wrap around my shoulders.

Love,

Dee Dee

Survival on the prairie was not easy. My parents and grandparents had survived the Great Depression. My Aunt Bernice endured the humiliation of being a "country kid" wearing a flour sack dress to school. Dad left the family farm to help win WWII as a soldier in the Philippines, where remembering the cattle and the farm he loved helped him survive the horrors he faced on the front lines. The harshness of prairie life offered no guarantees. It was a code of honor to survive whatever the prairie dished out: heat, drought, tornadoes, blizzards, war.

Yet, plastic pink flamingos stood in the midst of barometric turbulence and oppressive heat. For me, they symbolized the beauty of my mother's spirit. She cared enough to soften the harshness and add color to life in the front yard of her prairie home.

I really should put one on her grave and surround it with pink and white petunias, just in case God doesn't have plastic flamingos or petunias in heaven.

FLAMINGOS AND FLOWERS

Dear Mom,

Pink flamingos and pink petunias. Those were your yard decorating techniques on the farm: plastic, pink flamingo bodies stood right in front of the short white picket fence that guarded the pink and white petunias.

In the land of ducks, geese, mud hens and swans, we had plastic pink flamingos for our yard decorations. Distinctive, to say the least!

Flowers seemed like a luxury on the farm. You grew flowers in the garden, in an old metallic tub, along shrubs, and in rows next to the clothesline. Flowers were the beauty otherwise missing from the farm life; flowers were fragile, yet important to your sense of decoration. I remember going to the greenhouse in Webster, South Dakota, with you every spring to buy your flowers. Usually you bought white and pink petunias.

Flowers were important in another part of our lives. Every Memorial Day Grandma Olga, and Dad's sisters, Aunts Bernice and Lenore, and I would go to Fron Lutheran Church. We had a strong tradition to honor those veterans who died with memorial services and planting flowers on their graves.

A special flower among many that we placed on the Hauge graves is called a fern peony. It has the deepest red color and an incredible scent. Every time we went there, I smelled the peonies and counted blossoms—67 on Grandpa's plant one year. Grandma said that the people buried there were in heaven, so I associated the scent of the fern peonies with heaven. Smell the peony, think of heaven. We planted a peony on your grave. Its scent is just a reminder to me of where you are, Mom, but we left the pink flamingos in the store.

Love,

Dee Dee

As we come to terms with losing someone we love, we gain strength to face life on our terms. Similar to autumn, we shed much, like attitudes, lack of confidence, possessions, and sometimes, people. We have to let them go with dignity and in love, cherishing the difference they made in our lives.

However, a prairie autumn offers more than shedding; it provides a harvest of food and panoply of color. Autumn on the prairie is my favorite season. When the bright reds and flashing yellows surround me, I feel restored and soothed. The deeper reds and gold colors, in varying shades of bright and muted, form a colorful quilt that covers our farms and our communities.

Maybe God gives us the quilt of color to prepare for winter's cold. Maybe it is just that God knows change, though stressful, is good for us, and autumn's quilt comforts us.

Colorful comfort also came from the clothes that Mom

made and wore. Despite the rural environment, she cared about beauty and beautiful clothes. Her tall, slim figure looked great in the shirt-styled dresses that she made. She bought yards of brightly colored or pastel fabrics and Simplicity patterns at the department stores. Then she sewed dresses for church, holiday celebrations, and everyday wear. Her creations were stylish and enduring.

CLASSICAL ELEGANCE ON THE PRAIRIE

Dear Mom,

You were really a beautiful woman, Mom. I remember looking at your high school graduation picture and wanting to be as pretty as you were. You looked elegant in your white gloves, dresses, and hats. What I recall the best are your horn-rimmed glasses, your white skin, never tanned on the farm, and how tall you were.

I was tall as a child. Too tall, I felt. By eighth grade, I was probably 5'8", too tall and skinny, and I stood out in uncomfortable ways that I didn't like at all. You gave me advice, saying I would someday be glad I was tall because it would mean I could reach the top cupboard. I really didn't care about the top cupboard when I was the tallest girl in class and felt like a geek.

You wore beautiful dresses, Mom; clothes I am sure you made like that sleeveless, white shirtdress, button front with large red, blue, and purple polka dots. That was one of my favorite dresses. You were set with the addition of white gloves, white summer purse, and shoes with thin, tall heels.

I use the same purse 12 months of the year. When it wears out, I buy a new one. I don't even own a pair of white shoes, and the only gloves I wear are red leather that I bought for $1 at our *church rummage sale. They match my red Columbia coat, so I am set. I even feel somewhat fashionable.*

Fashion has changed a lot since you were on the farm, Mom. I think Jackie Kennedy influenced American women in wonderful ways by what she wore for clothes and accessories. Even on the farm, you were able to have a sense of classic elegance to match your beauty, Mom.

Love,

Dee Dee

Mom's sense of style was not limited to her alone. She also had a simple rule for us farm kids who caught lizards and frogs in bare feet and rolled in the hay bales: that there was no excuse for not looking our best for family gatherings and for church. We always dressed up when we went to Grandma's or attended church services. After all, those were the days of white gloves, white purses, white hats and even white handkerchiefs!

THE CHURCH ON THE PRAIRIE

Dear Mom,

Fron Lutheran Church has been an enriching part of our lives as the Hauge family church. Grandpa Hauge had helped re-build it after fire in 1942. As a child, I went there only for Memorial Day services and funerals. I married Kim there. We buried you there, Mom.

Although I grew up Catholic, I became Lutheran in college. I wanted to get married at Fron because I cherished the memories and feelings for the church. Do you remember May 14, 1976, Mom? I think you were happy that I was getting married, but the wedding photos depict a concerned look on your face. Were you worried or happy for me?

You so disliked cameras that I have very few pictures of you. We only had one family picture taken—ever, and very few casual group pictures that included you. You were elusive and hard to photograph.

Wedding photographs, now 24 years old, show a young woman and a young man in love. Family photos show young sisters who were a mere 10 years old, and others depict a mother, aunts and grandmothers no longer alive. All of these photos captured a historic moment in a small church on the prairie.

I have one photo of Fron Lutheran Church that I can see in my mind. It included Dad and all of your children at your grave, the day after your funeral. It was the hardest photograph I ever took.

Missing you,

Dee Dee

Whether durable pink flamingos, seasonal fall colors, or the historical church my ancestors helped build, my memories of prairie life will also endure. They are the foundation of who I am today, without the white gloves!

CHAPTER TEN

Spring

Sit quietly, doing nothing,
spring comes,
and the grass grows by itself.

Zen saying

Spring on the prairie brings bursts of color and fragrance. Spring is also a contradiction for me personally. New life emerges every spring with new calves and prairie flowers as I turn one year older.

TURNING 44

Dear Mom,

Today I turned 44. Friends and relatives flooded me with wonderful cards, telephone calls, and birthday wishes. I pampered myself with a massage, took Charlie for a drive in the country, and had lunch with Kelsey and Kim. It's been a great day, Mom.

Your sister Gennie bestowed my original birth announcement upon me after my daughter was born. It is a blue and pink floral "Baby is here!" announcement with your original handwriting. You wrote all my vitals: "7 lbs 4 ozs," "dk brown" hair with "blue" eyes." My birth announcement, in your handwriting, is one of my cherished possessions.

Dad's handwriting shocked me after your death. It was my first birthday after you passed on. Dad sent a card in his own handwriting on my first birthday without you, a first ever in my life. That was always your job, and you know how he wrote it, Mom? The envelope read, "Dee Dee Hauge." I'd been married for 13 years, and he wrote my maiden name.

Today is my 10th birthday without you. The first few birthdays without you were hard. Today I am 44, and it is great! Rick tried to make me feel old this morning, especially when he learned that Kelsey made me oatmeal for breakfast. Mom, nobody can make me feel bad about a birthday. I learned the hard way when you died that there is but one alternative to having a birthday. I'm not complaining; in fact, I am rejoicing and giving thanks for another year and another birthday. Thank you, God!

Love,

Dee Dee

Even though I got older every spring, the spring season seemed to renew Mom. I believe Mom loved spring the best because for her it was about tending and caring for the new. Dozens of baby calves were born every March and April. Red calves with white faces, black calves, loud bawling calves searching for their mothers. Springtime on the prairie meant white, purple, and pink blossoms: plum, apple, and chokecherry trees spewing forth their visual and scented proof of the season.

The abundance of prairie flowers astounds me. The virgin prairie of South Dakota produces a flower that I turned into many bouquets when I was a little girl. We called it the Mayflower. However, long ago the state declared this delicate purple crocus the state flower, and it's officially called the pasque.

I picked bouquets of Mayflowers for teachers and for Mom. It was an annual tradition like fasting from candy for Lent or dressing up for Easter services. Journeying through memories brought my loss of Mom to the forefront this particular Easter.

THE EMPTY EASTER EGGS

Dear Mom,

Easter break brought Jessie home from college for a visit. It is early Easter morning now and both girls sleep while I write to you. Life had been so hectic we hadn't even gotten out the Easter baskets and decorations. I thought I could let Easter slide by without the green grass and plastic eggs. After all, the girls are now 19 and 15, and I didn't think it would even really matter. We hadn't gotten the decorations out last year either, since we had Easter in San Diego. This holiday, important to me as a child, has become lost in the process of living a busy life, and being too harried to stop and decorate eggs.

Easter was so exciting when we were kids. We decorated eggs in purples, blues, oranges, and yellows. We baked and frosted Easter egg cookies. We had new dresses to wear for church. And after fasting from candy for all of Lent, we waited anxiously for the morning that ended the fast.

It was such a big thing, waking up on Easter morning when we were kids on the farm. Waiting to see what the Easter bunny brought was second only to Santa each year. It was candy, of course, but after six weeks of "no candy for Lent," it was a huge hit for us.

When I woke up this morning, I listened to a church program on TV. The minister was telling the story of a little boy who had learning disabilities. He was five years older than the other 19 children in class were, but he loved school and wasn't expected to live long, so the teacher allowed him to stay in school. Her Easter lesson for the children was to have them take a plastic egg home and bring it back filled with something about Easter. Most children brought flowers, rocks and butterflies back in their eggs. This little boy brought nothing, and the teacher knew he just hadn't caught on. When she went on to the next egg, the little boy asked her if she wasn't going to talk about what was in his egg as she had talked about the others' eggs. She said the egg was empty. He replied that Jesus' tomb was empty, and that was why his egg was empty. She realized then that he had understood Easter. When he died just a few months later, his peers covered his casket with 19 empty plastic Easter eggs.

This morning, my daughters will receive empty Easter eggs from me. Because I had nothing to fill the eggs nor put in their baskets, I pretended that Easter decorations and baskets meant very little to me. However, this morning, when I heard that story, I realized that the real meaning of Easter isn't just the decorations, but that the tomb was empty. The empty eggs in Jessie and Kelsey's baskets this morning represent that empty tomb. When life becomes too busy, we, too, can feel empty. We can feel like we have forgotten the important things. Important moments can slip by. We also feel empty when we go through struggles in life. We feel that no one is there for us, that no one understands. We feel empty inside, wondering if we will ever get to a better place.

Easter is about getting to a better place. Easter is about the times in our lives when we feel empty, that the struggles are too much, and then rejoicing as we rediscover our faith and know with certainty that God is there, in the form of His son, Jesus. Jesus' empty tomb symbolizes the hope we all need in this life.

Mom, I realized as I listened to the sermon, that this morning it will be the four of us here for Easter. We will go to church, have a turkey dinner, sit and talk and play a game or two. There may not be many more Easters with just the four of us waking up in our home on Easter morning. So I dug the decorations from the recesses of the space under the stairs. I had to show them that Easter is fun, filled with memories of baskets, artwork, and small wooden bunnies made over the course of their lives.

Jessie and Kelsey are no longer little girls excited to see what the Easter bunny brought. They are now teenagers who love the Lord whose tomb is represented by the empty eggs in their baskets. They are beautiful young women, Mom, who will enjoy the baskets you made for them when they were little girls. I am so glad that this Easter morning, Mom, I can celebrate it with my husband and daughters, empty Easter eggs and all.

Happy Easter, Mom!

The wonderful holiday of Easter changes dates every spring according to the church calendar. My journey through Easter memories brought to mind another date that never changes: April 2, 1971, the day our home was destroyed by fire. We lost everything that day. For all of us, especially Mom I imagine, the fire was a traumatic life marker, designating the before and after of instantaneous life change.

TREASURES LOST

Dear Mom,

It was a normal spring night on the farm. We were all in bed. Rick was off to college, so I had moved into his room, leaving my sisters to share the other bedroom. I loved to sleep in Dad's extra large, long-sleeved, white cotton shirts. Their heavy weave kept me warm and felt so good against my skin.

That's about all I was wearing when you came into my bedroom and told me to get up and get out, the house was on fire! It was 5:30 a.m., April 2, 1971.

Instinctively I dressed and grabbed the items sitting next to my bed on the floor, ready for school that day. I grabbed my small blue suitcase, which held clothes, drumsticks, and music.

You and Dad woke our nearest neighbors, Bonnie and Gary Strand, telling them our house was on fire. The old red fire truck seemed to drive painfully slow. All the while, this little girl was hoping the fire was out and we could return home soon.

When we returned a long 30 minutes later, we watched the northwest corner of the house—my old bedroom—burn down. Everything else was already gone. The New House of my dreams, the home of my family, every possession we ever owned, all destroyed. So was much of my spirit.

How was your spirit in that tortured moment, Mom? I can't imagine what it was like. Destroyed was the whole structure you built along with all that you had ever made, purchased, photographed, or enjoyed. The hand-crocheted bedspreads made by your mom; the beautiful clothes you sewed for us; and all of crafts you had made from delicate prairie flowers, gone!

I could not imagine how I would feel if I lost the treasured afghans you made for my daughters and all of our photographs of the girls when they were little and with you. It must have been extremely painful to lose all the evidence of our lives.

Love,

Dee Dee

One undeniable truth of spring is that after loss, each of us will face our internal renewal, an awakening of spring within ourselves. Whether it takes one month or nine years, we face our grief and move through healing because we are resilient human beings.

HAPPY MOTHER'S DAY

Dear Mom,

After Christmas, the hardest day of the year for me is Mother's Day. The first Mother's Day after your death was nearly impossible as I felt like an orphan. I am so grateful that Jessie and Kelsey showered me with wonderful cards, hugs, and lots of healing love.

Over the years, the cards from the girls are some of my most cherished artwork. A card of hearts with a very crooked "I LUV YOU" from Kelsey is framed art in my office. I tucked many of Jessie and Kelsey's cards into books I love to read. When I find them, it is pure joy, like the feeling I had finding a quarter in pants pockets on the farm.

Jessie is expressive in her writing. One of my cherished possessions is a 1998 Mother's Day card in which she wrote the following: "Without you, where would I be? Without you, I would not be who I am today. For I am made of and from you. Without you I would not be strong, I would not be kind, I would not have sense, I would not love. I am who I am because of you. You are a beautiful, strong, sensible, loving, kind woman. You are the wonderful woman I call my mother. I am who I am because of you."

Ditto, Mom. I am who I am because of you. With all my

heart, I say thank you, Mom. Happy Mother's Day!

Love,

Dee Dee

P.S. Jessie says Hi!

SECTION SIX

Mom's Heart

A mother is the truest friend we have,
when trials heavy and sudden, fall upon us;
when adversity takes the place of prosperity;
when friends who rejoice with us in our sunshine desert us;
when trouble thickens around us,
still will she cling to us, and endeavor by her kind precepts
and counsels to dissipate the clouds of darkness,
and cause peace to return to our hearts.

Washington Irving

CHAPTER ELEVEN

Connection Is The Key

*The best and most beautiful things in the world
cannot be seen or even touched.
They must be felt with the heart.*

Helen Keller

Mothers have an intuitive, virtually spiritual bond with their children. It is wired into nervous systems that mothers feel what children experience, almost reading their thoughts. We scan their eyes instantly and know their deepest secret. The physical and intuitive bond between a mother and her child provides a foundation of emotional connection. After a death, it takes time and focus to realize that the spiritual bond is never broken as long as a child remembers the journey.

PROOF OF MY CHILDHOOD

Dear Mom,

For years as an adult, I felt like I had no history since the house fire destroyed all of the photographs of our youth. I had nothing on film to show the life I lived, no photos as a little girl to compare to my girls and show them what I was like. No proof I was a tomboy, or wore dresses made by you and Grandma, or that I was Grandpa's girl. I had no evidence that I existed as a child—except for my memories.

I shared this thought with my cousin Roxie at a wedding reception. Her eyebrows creased in confusion when I first told her I had no photographs of me as a child. I reminded her that our house was destroyed by fire when I was young. Then her eyes opened wide in delight, and she recalled that her mother had a bunch of photos. Roxie said that she would sort through them for me.

I was hoping she would send them, excited even. True to her word, the packet arrived just a few months after the wedding. As I opened the package and saw proof of my childhood, my world shifted suddenly.

Images of my childhood stared back at me for the first time in ages. Reflections of me as a little girl, my family, my parents, me and my grandparents and cousins brought a torrent of tears. The emotions were incredible as I cried with joy. The floodgates of suppressed memories opened wide.

One picture in particular stood out, Mom. Grandma and Grandpa Weyer stood next to me on the farm with my long legs and short hair. I proudly posed with them as I had spent many days on their farm until I was six. To have photographic evidence of those very early years of my life was beyond my hopes.

Then I looked again. The Grandma and Grandpa were much younger than I remembered, and the house looked dirty, unlike I ever remember it. Then it struck me. The photograph was of you, Mom, standing next to Grandma and Grandpa at the front of a house dirtied from the Dust Bowl. You looked just like me. I had never realized that we looked alike, at least as children.

I could now show my daughters not only what I looked like as a kid, but what you looked like, too. What a blessing! What wonderful memories of being on that farm. How proud I was to think that at the same age, we both had the same long legs, the same tomboy look, and the same grimace from smiling into the sun for some relative's camera. We shared a lot more than I realized, Mom. That was one of the greatest gifts in the package from Roxie that day.

Love,

Dee Dee

I silently thanked Roxie for the photographs she unearthed for me. When the old photographs triggered the gushes of gratitude, perhaps I hadn't realized that the fire impacted me so traumatically as a child. Then, my mother's death reminded me of all of my losses through the years.

I would relax in bed at night, searching for a memory, like mining gold by chipping away with a rock hammer. The memories were vague, hidden deep, elusive. I longed for connection. The photographs provided that emotional link. Then I realized that I had imitated Mom in more than just looking like her.

CAN I SPIT HER IN THE EYE?

Dear Mom,

I never realized until after you died that we had our children at the same ages of 24 and 28. Why did you wait four years between children? For me, it seemed like a good idea as I enjoyed my time alone with Jessica during the first four years of her life.

You told me repeatedly that you were certain you were going to have a girl after you had Rick. You even knew the name: Dee Ann Marie. You often told the story of how you had Rick do things for "Dee Ann Marie," his soon-to-be little sister. You gave Rick baby dresses to put in "Dee Ann Marie's" dresser drawer, and asked him to do other things in preparation for "Dee Ann Marie." Rick was apparently well-trained to be a good big brother by the time I arrived.

I was born on March 14, 1956. About three days later, you brought me home from the hospital, placed me in the bassinet, and introduced me to my big brother. Rick looked at me, looked at you, and promptly asked you, "NOW can I spit her in the eye?"

Jessica was a bit more loving as an older sibling. She, like Rick, was nearly four when a sister came into her world. One night, about a month after Kelsey was born, Kim and I were relaxing in the living room while Kelsey was asleep and Jessie was playing in her room. Or so we thought. The next thing we knew, Jessie was proudly pushing her one-month old baby sister in her Strawberry Shortcake doll buggy. How had Jessica gotten her out of the crib by herself?! I was stunned, but the big sister smiled proudly at the feat and enjoyed pushing her baby sister in the doll stroller.

Mom, it is so much fun having two girls. They actually played with dishes, dolls, bears, and play dough: things I seldom did on the farm. Maybe it was the influence of having an older brother. I played with tractors, turning bread pans into wagons that hauled corn silage and hay. I played with cats, dressing them in dresses. Jessie did that with dogs, dressing Bitsy in winter boots and scarf, as if the husky were cold. I caught frogs, trapped for muskrats and did so many things that little girls do, I'm sure, when they had an older brother who wanted to spit in their eye when they were only three days old.

Love,

Dee Dee

Isn't parenting one of the ways that we learn about ourselves? Life is fully examined when we hold up a mirror and see ourselves for the first time. This happened for me when I had children. On some days, I look into their eyes and at their behavior, and I see myself. On other days, I see that I do the same things my Mother did. That shocks me because I swore I would never do those things!

As we journey through our memories, it's interesting to see what triggers the humor and laughter from our past. I woke up with mumps on both sides of my neck the morning my youngest sister was born. My care was up to Dad, and it was calving season, which meant he was not in the house much, and Mom was in the hospital for days. It's the epitome of helplessness turned into humor: real life situations that we each have where we learned, laughed and sometimes cried. Catching frogs with my brother made me laugh again and celebrate our closeness. Perhaps nicknames are emotional connections for you as they were for me.

DEE ANN MARIE

Dear Mom,

Dee Ann Marie was the name you gave me; and the name you used when you were mad. Most of the relatives on your side used that name.

Dee Dee was the nickname that Dad gave me early in my life, and we used it at home. Dee Ann was the name I used in school until I was 15.

During my first year in high school, around age 15, I thought that I should decide what name I wanted people to call me. I preferred Dee Dee, and I have been using it ever since.

In fact, all of us had nicknames. Rick was Doc for many years. Gayle was Corky. I had so many nicknames that at one point, I realized I would have answered to any one of seven names like Hollow Leg, Bottomless Pit, or Cackle.

Mom, one day you were just appalled at someone's new nickname for one of your children. In your exasperation, you said you should have named us kids Agatha or Gertrude so we would have had a good excuse for having a nickname.

No excuses needed, Mom. We just liked giving you a hard time, and nicknames were just one of many techniques we used!

Love,

Dee Dee

I like to think my mother's heart was behind all of her loving choices in how she parented her four children. I remember that we had a lot of freedom on the farm, or perhaps she was just too tired to chase after us. On the other hand, maybe she trusted us. I guess each of us remembers as we need to, or perhaps as we desire. The point is to make wonderful memories that sustain your heart connection, and bring in wit and comedy to make you smile.

PARENTING STRATEGIES THAT DIDN'T WORK

Dear Mom,

I had simple strategies for parenting. One was that having two kids meant there would be peace and harmony, versus the circus that the four of us children had on the farm. If there were only two children, then they would have to—certainly, they would WANT—to get along. There was no third person to turn to when the first sibling made you mad. The design was a "forced" friendship, and that would be a great deterrent to fighting.

I threw my theory out the window early on. Girls fight. It is that simple. Oh sure, they get along, but they also fight, over clothes, telephone time, and other silly, simple things.

Jessie would typically try to be the little mom and make everything okay. Kelsey was the pill. Her viewpoint focused on what was the benefit of being second in birth order. She used that knowledge to ensure that she did not appear to be the one who started the fight. She was more calculating than Jessie was. Jessie was always naive and walked right into such situations.

Occasionally, your son shows up to add fuel to the fire. Rick is the absolute master at getting the girls to fight. He knows exactly what to say and how to step back and watch the reactions quickly escalate into the fight.

I remember taking you shopping when we lived in Pierre, and the girls were about four and eight. They were fighting in the back seat of the car. How surprised you were that they would fight like that. Seems you had the same notion I had. I wonder where I got it!

Love,

Dee Dee

CHAPTER TWELVE

Recollections And Roots

There are two lasting bequests we can give our children:
One is roots. The other is wings.

Hodding Carter, Jr.

As I have sifted through my mental photographs remembering Mom, the connection has given me new footing. I found myself feeling stronger as I saw her strength and values. Recalling our roots, sifting through the mementoes of life together helps heal the heart. Often we surprise ourselves by what triggers the connection, even...

COOKIES

Dear Mom,

Tonight I'm making cookie dough for Kelsey's Sunday school class tomorrow. Her sixth-grade class is going to bake and frost heart-shaped cookies for the homeless shelter to celebrate Valentine's Day.

Cookies are an important part of my heritage. I remember the cookies you made. We baked, frosted, and let our mouths water in anticipation. Baking cookies with you was a joy; the time we spent was fun and heart-felt. Your cookies were a great snack, and I think the cookie jar was nearly always full. Occasionally we cheated and bought cookies, and Oreos were a great treat. But you usually baked the cookies we enjoyed.

I hate to admit to the importance of cookies in my life. After all, it is just a sugar treat. I have to confess, Mom, that I even made career decisions over cookies.

When Jessie was not quite two years old, I was facing a career decision. I had been part of a crazy newspaper world, oscillating from working fulltime to part-time. I drove to Sioux Falls, leaving Jessie with a baby sitter every day, just like millions of professional mothers everywhere.

Then one day, when I was debating about leaving my job, I

simply decided life was too short. I realized I had missed some of the best days of Jessie's short life. Most importantly, I had never baked chocolate chip cookies with my daughter. I had been busy in a career, but I had never had the time to bake chocolate chip cookies with her.

It was an easy decision to stay home. Perhaps it wasn't rational or logical, but then, I'm not sure there's anything rational about chocolate chip cookies. They're simply wonderful memory makers, and I needed to make some memories with my daughter, just as you had with your daughters. Life is too short to go without chocolate chip cookies. Right, Mom?

Love,

Dee Dee

Yes, we make memories together: one moment in time, heart to heart, word by word, shared bites of cookies. Do you cherish, as I do, those connections that families can create? The moments captured by our mental cameras are the glue that holds our lives together. I wonder what mental images my daughters will have of me?

It's a Mother's Right

Dear Mom,

One of the greatest joys I have as a mother is embarrassing my children. They make it so easy. Sometimes it takes nothing more than showing up, and they are red-faced. All I have to do is talk with one of their friends, and they want to die. I decided to up the ante, as it were, and find more creative ways to embarrass them.

I have found two excellent techniques that work well: singing and dancing. Now you recall how badly I sang, Mom. I once stood on a board that straddled two cement blocks in the basement, singing at the top of my lungs with my sister, wanting to sound so much better than she did. There wasn't a prayer. She had a voice; I did not. But I was competitive, and wanted to show you I could sing. You were the audience and stayed for the entire performance, even after the cats ran away.

The lack of skills does not deter me from thinking I should sing. After all, God gave me the desire to sing, Mom, just not the voice! In front of my daughters and their friends, I have crooned my own versions of sad, bad country songs that make no sense to anyone but me. I have belted out rock music to the public at large, through car windows, when we were on vacation. And I have tried to sing in church. Even that embarrasses my daughters.

The other way I embarrass my daughters is dancing. It requires coordination, which you did not give me genetically. Maybe it would have helped if I had been more physical on the farm, or if we had had sports for girls when I was in school. I simply have no gift of coordination. So when I dance, it's not a pretty sight.

I don't dance often unless I'm driving Kelsey somewhere. Then I dance. The other day I was dancing as I drove down Yellowstone Road in Cheyenne. Kelsey was trying very hard to ignore me, and then we stopped at a red light. She quickly assessed the embarrassment barometer—the degree to which anyone would recognize her with her mother—and relaxed when she learned that she did not know the people in the car next to us. Whew...she got by THAT time!

Occasionally, Mom, I combine the singing with dancing, such as when I perform what I call Moose Jiving. Now I know you're smiling as you try to imagine just how bad I look as I make matters worse.

Funny thing, Mom, is that I don't remember being embarrassed by you. I must have been, for I assume that every teenager is, but I can't recall it. Maybe you were just a cool mom, and I truly am just a geek!

Love from the Geek!

Dee Dee

Celebrating the humor can deepen your roots as they did mine. My friend decided to make a list of a few questions that she never asked her mother. Her questions centered on the mysterious habits she observed but never mentioned.

- I was worried sick about you. Why didn't you ever explain that all those incidents of sweat and fatigue were hot flashes?

- What did you do with the five sizes of clothes in your closet through 50 years?

- I notice you've kept those good hats on the top shelf of your closet for 20 years. Why did you cherish them?

- Why did you confess to hating fish after Dad died? Moreover, why did you eat his catches every Friday night for 52 years?

- Why wouldn't you ever buy asparagus if it was priced over $2.35 per pound?

What questions, no matter how trivial, would you ask your Mom so that you could know her better? What peculiarities or habits come to mind that you would like to understand? This question lingered in my head for many years.

DID YOU CRY?

Dear Mom,

Did you cry when I left for college? I barely remember leaving. I graduated from high school on May 19, 1974, and began college in the June summer session. I was off to my new adventure, away from the small town atmosphere that seemed so confining at the time. I had declared music as my major and wanted to start lessons early to get a head start on my college career. Rick was going to summer school as well, so I felt safe heading off to college early.

I can't remember any of your emotions when I graduated from high school and went to college. Were you sad, happy, or relieved? I suspect the latter was most accurate. Were you afraid for me? Did you share the same fears I have for Jessie? I worry about her walking across campus at night alone after class. She loves night classes and the full load it affords her, but I worry about her safety. Did you worry about the decisions I made? Were you so used to my mistakes that you figured some more wouldn't hurt me?

Were you proud of me, Mom? Did you see me having the potential to do great things? Were you proud when I played in the Pride of the Dakotas marching band? Were you proud that I graduated from college?

It is funny what we remember. Maybe I do not recall your feelings because you didn't express them. However, they must have been there. You must have felt some of the same fears, joys, and pride that I feel for Jessie.

I cried when Jessie went to college, Mom. Did you cry when I left?

Love,

Dee Dee

It takes courage to recall your life with your mother: to remember the touching events, the incidents that brought tears, words that you regret, decisions you wish you'd thought through more carefully. *All* feelings are wonderful keys to unlock your roots.

I Miss You Mom

Dear Mom,

Jessie loves college, but she misses us. She called one night, at 1:30 a.m. In tears she said, "I miss you, Mom!"

How many times have I said, "I miss you, Mom," since you died? How many times have I looked at your photographs, your ornaments, made your recipes? How many times have I gone to Roslyn, visited Fron, or driven out to the farm and said, "I miss you, Mom?"

I don't know how many times, but I will tell you something. When Jessie called me and said she missed me, her words, "I miss you, Mom," touched my heart and made me feel very special.

123

I hope you can hear me, Mom. I miss you.

Love,

Dee Dee

I cannot emphasize enough the freedom I felt when my burden of grief lifted. I soared as I wrote letters. I could see the light again, and I reclaimed all the good memories for my mental scrapbook. In those moments when I think I am falling into grief again, I read my letters. I write again. I remember my scrapbook called Celebration, and I close my eyes, flipping through the memories.

The narrative healing process helps us attain that freedom. Those who lose loved ones need to remember the good times to help lighten their load. Be nurtured by your recollections and your roots, and claim all the values and love you received from the one you loved and lost.

Life
On
The Farm

Do more than belong, participate.
Do more than care, help.
Do more than believe, practice.
Do more than be fair, be kind.
Do more than forgive, forget.
Do more than dream, work.

William Arthur Ward

CHAPTER THIRTEEN

Reality Is Just Perceptions

We do not see things as they are.
We see them as we are.

The Talmud

Prairie life in South Dakota honors traditions and salutes our ancestry and values. Although influenced by tradition, each family is unique when choosing their perceptions that guide their tasks and families. For example, my dad was close to the land and animals all of his life. He gauged weather changes by the clouds, the wind, and the arthritis in his knee.

My mother's reality was to be thrifty and economical from sewing our clothes, growing and harvesting fresh vegetables, and making our Christmas ornaments. She also valued neighborly kindness, whether to a stray dog, a newborn calf, or someone who was stranded by their broken down car.

STRAY DOGS AND CATS

Dear Mom,

Stray dogs and cats: remember how we used to acquire stray animals on the farm? People would dump their pets in the country, assuming some farm family like us would take them in, feed and care for them.

We did. We acquired some of our best pets that way. Do you remember the black and white dog that showed up one day? Dad named him Nixon because he was "good for nothing."

Our farm was a great playground of animals and kids. Dogs always seemed to be in the mix. Cats would come and stay. At one time, I counted over 20 cats to play with on the farm.

I admired how you cared for animals that were suffering. One time a "mommy cat" died after having her kittens that were probably two weeks old at the time. You took the kittens and fed them cow's milk from a medicine dropper. They survived, and we christened the one we adopted "Lucky." Lucky was around a long time and was definitely one of the cats that used nine lives in her years on the farm.

Jessie is kind of like you, Mom; she loves strays—in the form of people. She takes in people that are less fortunate and cares for them. One Thanksgiving she was driving in town after dinner when she saw a homeless person. She came home, put together an entire grocery bag of leftover food, and took it to him. Unfortunately, he was gone when she returned, but the gesture was a caring one.

Jessie took in friends who lacked decent homes or were going through tough times—kind of like on the farm when we had bad weather. We lived at a place where we were the first farm on a long stretch of road. People with car trouble walked south and found us first. We never turned anybody away and welcomed perfect strangers into our homes. Our clothes went to babies not dressed for a South Dakota spring blizzard. Strangers made telephone calls on our lines and Dad's tractor pulled cars out of ditches. We simply took care of people who needed help.

You would be proud of Jessie, Mom. She has a very caring spirit about her, a very sharing spirit. I think she inherited that from you.

Love,

Dee Dee

THE WEATHER KNEE

Dear Mom,

As I sit in my hotel room in Cody, Wyoming, watching television, I think about the first TV we had. I'll bet most people, including your granddaughters, have no concept of tubes and rabbit ears.

We had one of the first televisions in Liberty Township: a huge box with a screen that projected black and white images. I remember when my friend's family got a color TV. That was a big deal, and it was cool to go over there and watch it.

Do you remember some of our old shows, Mom? I Love Lucy, Leave It to Beaver, Bonanza, *and* The High Chaparral. *Walter Cronkite was a trusted nightly visitor, and news was something we took seriously.*

Sometimes I wish I had lived in the era of old radio for the creative experience of listening to the dramatic shows with no video. We would have painted mental pictures, and I'll bet you had to listen attentively, didn't you Mom? More importantly, you listened to some of the great programs, newscasters, and entertainers of all time: Edward R. Murrow, Jack Benny, Milton Berle, and Lawrence Welk.

The news and weather warnings on the radio were critical for farm life. Transistor radios held a guarantee. Even though we'd lose electricity, we always had transistor radios that kept us in tune with the world. Dad was a faithful listener to WNAX, Yankton, South Dakota, and KFGO, in Fargo, North Dakota, for the weather.

Weather was the enemy, the blessing, the curse, and the benevolent donor to life on the farm. The weather gaveth; the weather tooketh away. I remember listening to the TV for tornado warnings in the summer. How quickly we could descend to the southwest corner of the basement when we heard tornado warnings. I remember blizzard warnings, temperatures, wind speed, and barometric pressure readings, all critical to survival on the prairie.

Of course, Dad did not rely on television as we did for weather. He relied on his knee. He would say his knee hurt and that the weather was changing. Knee hurt, weather was changing. It was a frequent saying, one that I never believed. He was the teaser, after all, and I was getting older and beginning to catch on. I wasn't going to be the sucker who believed THAT story.

Imagine my embarrassment on the day I watched the science teacher on TV describe how barometric pressure affected joints, like the knees, and how much joints hurt when the weather was changing. Dad was right!

Radio and later television brought us the world. We had farm magazines, the Watertown Public Opinion *and the* Webster Reporter and Farmer. *That was our media world. Our news sources, our conduit to great thinking, great political storms, and great events off the farm.*

Love,

Dee Dee

Our family values launch us into adulthood with enthusiasm and naiveté. The world is truly an oyster where the young discover their pearls of wisdom through relationships, adversity, and learning.

DATING

Dear Mom,

Last night we took Kelsey and her boyfriend out for dinner. It was cute watching them enjoy each other's company shyly in front of us. The poor guy spilled his glass of soda in his nervousness. He has the same big brown eyes of Charlie, our golden retriever.

Remember some of the guys I dated? On my first real date, I brought home this person to meet you when Aunt Stella roared from the kitchen, "Bring him on in here, Dee Dee. We'll check him out!" I was embarrassed horrendously. Stella had struck again.

You helped me deal with breaking up with one boyfriend—in your casual way. I came home so sad, describing the breakup to you, sure of my shattered heart. It was the first and only time I shared that intimacy with you. After listening carefully to my long, sad story, you made one profound comment: "Well, there are more fish in the sea."

There are many fish in the sea. I have actually used that line with my daughters in jest, saying, "That was the only advice I ever got from my mom, so don't expect much more from me." Then they clobber me because they know better.

I do talk with my daughters a lot, and I talk with their friends, too. I want to understand these kids, know how they think, and tell them that they are good stuff. So few people support kids today and actually spend time with them. Every kid needs a caring adult, and I try to be that for my daughters' friends.

The other day Kelsey told me that all of her friends think I am cool. I was so honored, Mom. I don't try to be cool. I just try to be there for her friends, listen to them, and help them. Maybe, occasionally, I succeed.

Love,

Dee Dee

If we can learn from our mistakes, then we mature with wisdom, and each generation can support the next. However, I am sometimes at a loss to explain random acts of violence to Mom in the next world or my children in this one. We embrace it and weep; we abhor it and turn away. How should we perceive this reality?

MATTHEW SHEPARD'S MOM

Dear Mom,

Some things mothers should never have to do. One is burying their children. Two is seeing their child's bludgeoned, bloody face after a merciless attack. Three is having their private affairs made a public spectacle filled with hate, vicious attacks, and worldwide media coverage. I will explain what happened.

Two men savagely beat a University of Wyoming student, Matthew Shepard. Then they tied him to a wooden fence and left him to die about 50 miles from here. A biker found him and called for help. An ambulance took Matthew to a hospital in Ft. Collins, Colorado. His parents, living in Saudi Arabia, received the phone call and flew immediately to see Matthew. He died within a few days from severe damage to his brain.

When I heard the story, my first thought was for the mother. A mother should never get that phone call, nor see a child she brought into this world savagely destroyed by another human being. A mother should never have to fly across the world to find her child unrecognizable.

I thought of you, Mom, as I cried for Matthew's mother and all mothers. I cried for the pain only a mother can know. I cried when I saw people showing up in the name of God, criticizing her son. I cried when I saw people in angel costumes, praying for peace and when I saw the fence posts and the funeral procession. I cried for the pain of the mother, fearing I would ever face the same tragedy. Deep in my heart during that tragedy, I felt the strength of all women's hearts, especially from my family.

Grandma Olga was a strong woman. She lived to be 95, dying just five months before you did. Unlike you, though, she buried two of her children, Lenore and Carvel. I always wondered how she could be so strong. Her daughter Lenore suffered from cancer, as did her dad. It must have been hard to watch her die, and then bury her near her father's grave at Fron Lutheran Church Cemetery.

I do not think parents burying children at any age is in keeping with the natural progression of life. It feels unfamiliar and backward in the life sequence. Even so, it is reality, and Grandma Olga dealt with it in her strong Norwegian style.

By the way, did I tell you Matthew Shepard was gay? That was the reason for the beating, the reason people showed up in the name of God to call him a "faggot." Mom, I didn't care that Matthew Shepard was gay. I simply saw parents grieving over a tragic loss, and a mother doing things she should never have to do.

Love,

Dee Dee

When perceptions clash and reality seems harsh for our hearts, we feel vulnerable. Vulnerability is good and allows a flushing of the pain we carry through tears, writing, kindness, or anger at injustice. Vulnerability breeds strength and resilience. After such deep cleansings of the soul, we return to the familiar to comfort us.

THE COMFORT TABLE

Dear Mom,

The basement of the New House was where you did the laundry using the old wringer washing machine. We made stuffed German sausage that Dad called "wurst" down there as well, and stored miscellaneous items from the Old House.

Among those miscellaneous items were a round, solid oak table, handmade cabinet and cradle Gayle and I played with, and the solid oak secretary with the curved glass door. The antiques were downstairs because they were just old furniture back then. They weren't valued as quality, solid oak, or master crafted, or as beautiful pieces of wooden furniture carrying family history. They were just from the Old House, and we relegated them to the status of basement furniture.

I have spent much of my adult life searching for replicas of those pieces. I had the chance to buy a round, solid oak table and eight chairs for $350. I called Bernice to see if that was a good price. She calmly said, "Yes, Dee Dee, that is a very good price. Besides, there's nothing more comforting than sitting at a round, oak table."

My girls ate at that table with you. They baked cookies and cooled them there. Our family gathered at special family holidays around that table.

*I sat at the table, alone, just days after you died. I
remembered Bernice's words now as clearly as I did then. The
round oak table comforts, soothes, and reminds me of my family,
present and past. What a tremendous blessing from just an old
piece of furniture.*

Love,

Dee Dee

HOLDING TREASURES

Dear Mom,

*I really wanted an antique, solid oak secretary. I wanted the
same kind you had—one with a curved glass door, three drawers,
and a pull-down desktop with spaces to put papers and bills, like
Dad had done on the farm. That pull down top hid treasures for
me to explore and play with, unknown to you and Dad, or so I
thought.*

*The secretary that I wanted to hold my treasures was
expensive. I finally found one I could afford, priced at $550. I
negotiated the price to $500, and told Kim it would make a
wonderful Christmas present. Since I had just purchased fishing
gear for him, I wanted him to present it to me. I mentioned this
quite a few times, telling him I really wanted the secretary for
Christmas.*

*I traveled out of town for work in early December, and Kim
used that occasion to take Jessie and Kelsey, who were then 10
and 6, to the country antique store to buy the present. The price
of $550 was still on the price tag, so Kim had to negotiate the
price down again, knowing I felt $500 was fair. As soon as he
started negotiating, the girls feared he wasn't going to buy. They*

tugged at his arms, saying repeatedly, "But Dad, it's the ONLY thing Mom wants for Christmas! We have to get it!" He paid $550 for the secretary.

I spent hours exploring the secretary on the farm, Mom. It is where I played with Dad's WWII medals. The Bronze Stars and Purple Heart meant nothing to me as a child, but they were pretty, and I knew they were Dad's. Today, I keep family photos, treasured tablecloths, and antique dishes in my secretary. It is a great place for holding treasures.

Love,

Dee Dee

I'm glad furniture can provide comfort and hold treasures that nurture and nourish. The old, worn table and secretary, both made of oak, share a combined durability, and reassure me that I won't forget the same lessons offered by the treasures they hold. Do you have a special piece of furniture that comforts you?

CHAPTER FOURTEEN

Legacies

*Blessed are those who can
give without remembering
and take without forgetting.*

Elizabeth Bibesco

My mom's legacies appeared in memories as an intricate pattern of her crocheted doilies, creatively woven with patience and enjoyment. As I traveled back through my journey of memories, I also weaved this delicate tapestry of the whole woman I called mother with her faults and gifts, Depression culture and prudence, creative talents, and loving care of her family.

I've shared with you the family traditions and principles that shaped her, but she was also honed by the prairie, itself a tapestry of color, wildlife and weather. Within her sheltered world of family, surrounded by prairie, gardens, pink flamingos, and children, she exuded strength of generations. Her strength was the foundation of her legacy.

Any mother's influence is pervasive, shaping children as the winds carve the land. I discovered mother's strength in me as I searched through Christmas ornaments, read old letters, plowed through Roxanne's box of family mementoes. One way that I celebrated Mom's legacies was by searching for antique items of my past like Mom's dishes.

DUZ SOAP DISHES

Dear Mom,

Duz dishes is what Rick called the antique Golden Wheat china I served dinner on one night. You collected that set of dishes, Mom, from boxes of Duz Soap. Beautiful wheat designs on cream china, with gold rimmed edges. They were the "good" dishes, collected from boxes of soap. Of course, the house fire destroyed them, but their memory lingers.

On my journey of exploring the past, those dishes triggered an antique hunt urge in me. I thought about collecting them as I did a set of dark green Depression dishware for Jessie. Every time she played in the piano contest at Gettysburg, South Dakota, we would go to the local antique shop afterwards and buy some more dark green dishes as her reward. I've promised to actually give them to her...someday!

It wasn't so much that I wanted the wheat dishes, as I desired to explore the memory. How beautiful were they in your eyes? What pride and joy did you feel when you served one of your delicious meals on those plates? It was special to you, and I wanted to capture that feeling in my hunt for the dishes. I filed the desire away in the category of "Someday I'll...." get around to collecting those cherished dishes.

Finding three plates for 25 cents at a rummage sale got me started. I decided to pursue the dream of collecting the dishes you loved. The hunt was on, and I savored it. I showed the dishes to Jessie and Kelsey and shared what they meant to me. Only two weeks later, I found the complete set at a flea market for just $68, but I could not buy them.

Buying the dishes would mean the hunt would be over, and I couldn't handle that thought. Jessie was with me, and she thought I was crazy not to buy the set. In fact, she returned to the shop and discovered a 10 percent discount. I told her I'd think about it. Buying them would eliminate the joy I felt in hunting for them.

Well, my daughters purchased and presented me with those dishes for Christmas that year. I cried. I now own the complete set of Duz dishes in their South Dakota wheat stemmed beauty. They remind me of the flowing, glistening wheat fields blowing in the prairie breeze, and all the great food you served to your family with those loving hands for so many years.

Thank you Mom!

Maybe Mom had no choice but to get free dishes from Duz boxes of soap. However, I admire the simple beauty of golden wheat stems on the china that adorns my antique hutch. The dishes are simple reminders of the wonderful prairie life that influenced my family for generations.

MISSING THE PRAIRIE

Dear Mom,

I've been living in Wyoming now for four years. Two days ago, I drove across the state and saw the beautiful mountain vistas capped in snow, with clear, crisp blue skies. Bright sunshine sparkled on the snow. It was a gorgeous day.

Yet, Mom, the older I get, the more I miss the prairie. I took it for granted when I lived there and did not appreciate the colors of the grasses and even the weeds until I was in college. Then, Kim was studying dendrology and the colors that foliage turns. When he said even prairie grasses turn colors, I thought he was crazy. I knew and loved the fall colors on the maples, oaks, chokecherry, and Russian olives, in reds, oranges, browns, and silver. I'd never realized that the colors of the grasses changed in the fall just like the leaves on the trees.

Next to fall foliage, I miss water the most in Wyoming. Growing up on the farm, it wasn't a pool we jumped in to cool off after a hot day. It was Pickerel Lake, home to our cabin, many family picnics, and days of playing in the clean, cool water. We must have seemed like fish to you. I really don't recall ever being afraid of the water, especially in my bright yellow ducky inner tube with an orange duck head. Then I graduated to the bigger inner tubes, and delight of delights, the tractor inner tube. Do you remember that, Mom? It was so large that we stood on it, balanced, and dived or jumped off it into the lake. It was big enough for about six people to hang onto, and it gave us great speed in eluding water fights.

I had enormous fun on the water as a child. Even as an adult, I've been near water all of my life until living in Wyoming. Kim and I have lived near the Big Sioux River at Sioux Falls, the Split Rock Creek at Garretson, and then, at Roy Lake. Once we moved to Pierre, we were only a three-minute walk from the shores of the Mighty Mo, the Missouri River, and just a short 10-minute drive to Lake Oahe.

Mom, you would enjoy a great lake like Lake Oahe. I don't think you spent much time there with us, as you never were a boat or water person. Our girls grew up waterskiing, boating, floating, swimming, and fishing on Lake Oahe. Friends gathered and we shared beers, campfires, and created wonderful memories on the shores of Lake Oahe.

A favorite memory was the first time Jessie water-skied. Giving her motherly advice from my own experiences, which included wrecks on Pickerel Lake, I told her to keep her knees bent. I meant as she got up on skis. She took me literally, got up, and kept her knees bent the entire time. I wish I had that one on video: this tall, skinny girl skiing on Lake Oahe with bent knees. At least she skied!

The Glacial Lakes of northeastern South Dakota will always be my home, Mom. Water is just too important to live in a dry area forever!

Love,

Dee Dee

Outdoor recreation was integral to our family life when I was a child and as my children grew up. Despite my mother's resistance to the idea of ever getting into the water herself, she always encouraged us to be active, take risks (as long as we had our life jackets on!), and try hard. This legacy of good advice stood the test of my endeavors as a child and well into my career.

LEARNING TO SHARE

Dear Mom,

You have no idea what I do for a living. I'll bet you never attended an adult learning seminar on leadership, public relations, or customer service. I'm sure you never wrote a press release, edited stories or created promotional plans. I wonder how I got into this career! I do know that you raised a successful group of people. You instilled confidence in those early years that we developed fully as adults. You inspired in us a desire to get ahead and to do better. We all want to improve our lot, and see life be better for the next generation.

Be proud, Mom. None of us is wealthy monetarily, but we are rich in the fullest sense. We have fulfilling careers where we can make a difference. We care. We are dedicated, and we are grounded persons.

There is one thing you taught us that is the fundamental reason why we're doing so well. You taught us to share, not to be selfish, but to take what we have and share it with others. We are all doing that in our careers in one way or another, thanks to you teaching us that value.

Now I get the chance to share my life experiences and my skills with other people in my seminars and consulting practice. I am so lucky to share the best, to inspire, to help people get to a better place. I carry on a tradition you inspired in us a long time ago.

Love,

Dee Dee

Because my mother and dad lived through the Depression, they were careful and frugal with resources. It is interesting how that experience translated through the years as simplicity in our lives, making do with what we had and recycling everything into something. As a small child, I never had thoughts of being poor. Rather, I felt abundant then, and I still do today.

KEEPING THE PLEASURES OF LIFE SIMPLE

Dear Mom,

"Keep the pleasures of life simple" is my personal motto, one I use in my training seminars as well as in every day life. It is borne of experience, sadness and expectations unfulfilled, and yet it frees me to live in this moment, of this day, every day. I'll explain.

I found myself going to Tokyo for the third time in six months in 1995. I was on a sales mission for South Dakota Tourism with United Airlines, and then with Northwest Airlines. I coordinated South Dakota's part of the opening of the replica of Mt. Rushmore built near Imaichi-city north of Tokyo.

Life was busy with two daughters and Kim's job moving full speed ahead. I bought a book on simplicity in life in the Minneapolis airport. The book helped me regain my perspective about my busyness. I read and re-read it, underscored and highlighted most of the text. Mostly, I have tried to apply the principles in the book.

I think simplicity is a highly desirable state and is difficult to achieve. Simplicity is threatened by media clutter—the millions of messages we are bombarded with every week. Simplicity is threatened by not knowing ourselves—being unfocused, unclear about goals. Moreover, simplicity is threatened by the American dream of getting ahead and always having the ability to acquire more stuff of greater status.

A friend in Pierre taught me a valuable lesson about simplicity, once saying that whatever amount of money you have, it would never be enough, because every time you earn more, there are more ways to spend it. Thinking about that was depressing, because I always assumed that once I was not "poor," I would be okay and have what I needed. I had never thought about being in the trap of always chasing something with a greater dollar sign.

Then, I went to Tokyo for the third time in six months and realized that working hard and chasing the great dream was not bringing me happiness. The job was wonderful, a true blessing in my life. Yet I had to remember to take pleasure in the simple, everyday delights, instead of delaying that pleasure or making it contingent on always having more, bigger, or expensive.

You left me that value, Mom, of the joy of simple pleasures: the taste of a great apple pie or the smell of spring flowers on the prairie. We delighted in the joy of clouds shaped like animals in the sky, newborn calves, and kittens and puppies on the farm. Most of all, we relaxed in the peace from the vibrant and masterful colors of a South Dakota prairie sunset.

All of those pleasures are free. You cannot buy a sunset or influence the shape of clouds. The apple pie is there for the tasting, and the flowers have existed forever on that prairie. All it takes is the mindset that those are wonderful gifts, very special pleasures. Simple pleasures, free for our enjoyment. Of all the lessons, you taught me, Mom, this is perhaps the best, as it is the basis of the rest of my life. It gives me permission to slow down, regain perspective, and know what is truly important.

Thank you, Mom.

As I continued my narrative healing journey, I realized that Mom lived vicariously through me. I had no greater delight than to amaze her with my travels to places she could see in her mind as I described them. In turn, she was a patient listener and my best cheerleader. Everyone needs a cheerleader in life. Sometimes, when we lose the person who most supports us, we mature into the role ourselves. Have you noticed?

A SAFE PLACE TO BRAG

Dear Mom,

I've been a lucky person in my career. I've had four wonderful jobs in media, travel, and banking and now with my own business. I wasn't just lucky in terms of the job or the opportunities they presented. I was lucky to have you and your support. You were, after all, a very safe person to whom I could brag.

I didn't always appreciate that support. I took for granted telling you about some of the trips I took. After all, your worldly travel experiences included journeys in South Dakota, Minnesota, North Dakota, Montana, and Iowa. When I traveled, it was to Florida, New Orleans, and Detroit—much more glamorous than your small world. You told me once that you lived through my career, that there was no need for you to travel. Yes, I did it for you, and you enjoyed hearing about it from me. You gave me permission to brag.

In October of 1990, I learned that I was going overseas to Japan for the first time in my life. I called home to tell you about it. We were so excited, then Dad got on the phone, and he was silent. He fought the Japanese in WWII and took no delight in his daughter flying there for any reason.

I came home from the trip and called you right away. It changed my life: how I saw the world, the measure of how I thought life should be lived. I shared all of that with you. You were a safe place to brag, Mom. I could tell you my stories and feel proud because you were proud. I was doing well, and I knew that you knew it. It was great having you share my career and my growth.

Then you died just a few weeks later, in early December. One month later, I attended a follow-up meeting to the Asian sales mission in Denver. I was meeting people with whom I had flown, eaten, and walked many miles over the course of a two-week sales mission. These people had become friends in Japan.

No one in the group looked different, but I felt different. My mom had just died. I was numb, still forcing my mind to focus. But I carried on with business, and got back on the plane to come home that night.

The plane ride to Pierre was disaster. I started crying, couldn't stop, and didn't know why. Then it hit me: I realized that would be my first flight when I couldn't call you and tell you about my trip. I had lost my safe place to brag.

You filled many roles in life, Mom, but one of the most important was your pride in me. It gave me permission to be the best I could be. You were always proud, and I knew that. Knowing that truth empowered me, making what I did worth the effort. I did much of it for you, the woman who had traveled only as far as Montana, once in her life.

Love,

Dee Dee

Have you lost someone, yet weeks or months later found yourself reaching for the telephone to call and ask a question or share an impression? If you've lost your mom, you understand. Countless times I've reached for the phone, thinking I'd ask Mom how to make her frosting, can her pickles, or just tell her about a recent trip. My fingers still want to dial 486-4356 and have just one more conversation.

CHAPTER FIFTEEN

Celebrating

The kiss of the sun for pardon,
The song of the birds for mirth,
One is nearer God's heart in a garden
Than anywhere else on Earth.

Dorothy Frances Gurney

I have titled this final chapter *Celebration* because I truly can celebrate my mother's passing with joy now. You will find in my final letters that I arrived at that ending stage of grieving called acceptance, and I learned some hard lessons along the way.

Often there is a misconception about arriving at this stage, or in fact, dealing with grief at any stage. As people seek solace, they might believe that the journey of healing means not feeling the hurt anymore. The word closure means a conclusion or resolution. Those seeking closure to loss may think that an end to grief means an end to the pain of emptiness.

I have not found that to be true for me or others who have lost a family member. The heart still feels an ache, though time may dull the ache or lessen the heartbreak to a twinge. The only way to begin the healing process is to take the first step. Grab a pen and paper and write your first letter. The truth is that I feel an ache and joy at the same time. I celebrate Mom's life, sometimes with poignancy and at other times with genuine humor.

TOLERANCE FOR PAIN

Dear Mom,

You had an incredible tolerance for pain. It must have been the tough German, deny-all-pain part of you. I recall when you were sick in the Old House, and had surgery after tolerating days of pain. People didn't just go see the doctor back then. They only went after trying all other options.

En route to my eight-month prenatal check-up in Watertown, I stopped to see you and Dad. You were in an incredible amount of pain. I called my doctor to ask if I could bring you with me, and he agreed. I had you in Watertown an hour later, and you were in surgery an hour after that. You had an obstructed bowel, a very painful condition. Again, I have no idea how you tolerated so much pain, or why, but I suspect it was because it was supposed to be in your life.

The day you died was the last day you tolerated such pain. You were hurting all day, Dad said, but he had no idea how badly. You hid pain from him very well. Turns out you probably had heart attacks all day. When you finally agreed to let Dad take you to the doctor, it was too late. You died of a heart attack in the hospital bed.

I do not have your tolerance for pain, Mom. I think you were raised in an era of few options and demands for tolerance. I was raised in an era of solutions borne by prescriptions and doctors. Maybe the lesson in life is that there is a healthy balance between the two.

Love,

Dee Dee

The key to celebrating the good in all of your memories is the acceptance of all feelings. Acceptance enables one to be free.

SAYING GOODBYE

Dear Mom,

The hardest thing I've had to do in my life is say goodbye to you. I didn't get to say goodbye when you were alive and could respond to me with a hug or your tender smile. I whispered goodbye to you when I saw your body in the casket.

I don't remember much about the period after you died until the funeral. After the phone call, I tried to pack clothes for the trip in molasses-like slow motion. The next morning, Kim drove us home in record time, and I wore sunglasses indoors to hide my swollen eyes. That night in Roslyn I walked with Dad and asked him how old you were. I was startled to learn you were only 62. I'd never known your age. Then I learned that Dad was 68. Then it hit me: I was half Dad's age and we had both just lost our moms.

I helped pick out the flowers for your casket and was disappointed at not being able to have the hymn you most loved at your funeral. I shook at the service and everyone asked me if I was cold. I wasn't; I just couldn't quit shaking.

At the lunch after the funeral, a dear friend came up to me, held my hands, and said, "You never got to say goodbye." I fell into his arms and sobbed. He was the first person to identify the feelings that were killing me inside.

I was never good at saying goodbye. I can watch a movie with goodbyes and cry. I cry at the thought of saying goodbye to a friend who is moving away, a dying pet, or to any kind of loss. However, I cried for years at not being able to say goodbye to you, and in effect, truly wishing you a safe journey.

I do not want to lose anyone that way again. I know I don't have a choice, but if I did, no matter how difficult, I would want

*to be there to say goodbye at the end. Then maybe the crying
wouldn't last so long.*

Love,

Dee Dee

I thank God I was finally able to say goodbye to Mom
through writing letters. When I first started the journey
through memories, I noticed that I mostly wanted to talk
about the emptiness of those first Christmas seasons
without Mom. Her absence was palpable. As I progressed,
I uncovered stories of humor and values that lifted my
spirits. That's when I knew I started looking forward instead
of behind me.

JUST ONE MORE DUCK DINNER

Dear Mom,

*I think all good cooks have their best dish, a special recipe
they may have received from their mom or created on their own.
Perhaps the dish is seasonal, traditional, or rarely served. The
best dish is a recipe for a special food that conjures up memories
of great meals, served with pride and love in gatherings of
friends and family. The best dish is a gift from the person who
prepares it for those who still taste the magnificence on their
tongues.*

*For some, the best dish may be lasagna, or German noodles
or another ethnic dish. For others, it's a recipe handed down
through the generations for soup or chicken. You prepared the
duck recipe like no one else, to the pleasure of many hunters and*

family members over your lifetime of cooking.

Last weekend, a friend of ours from Brookings stayed overnight on his way to Colorado. He has been our friend since college, and we were retelling stories of hunting and fishing weekends near Roslyn. He mentioned that no one made a perfect duck dinner as you did.

I wish I had kept track of how many people have told me that no one made duck as you did. It was sumptuous: slowly roasted with a strong sage dressing, using homemade bread, giblets, and onions, served with squash, baked potatoes and a salad. Many hunters enjoyed your great meal over the years.

Some say that women marry our fathers. In at least one way, I married my Dad, as Kim hunts. When ducks filled our freezer, I had to figure out how to cook them. When I implored you to send me the recipe, I knew you did not have one. You agreed to write it down the next time you made one, and the instructions came in a letter graced with your humor.

"Dear Dee Dee,

"Here's how you make duck. First, shoot the duck. Next, pluck the feathers. Then clean out the insides….." *and on it went in your humorous style.*

I laughed when I read your opening line. I was determined to prepare a duck dinner as well as you. Somehow, I secretly longed for all the compliments you had received all the years. But a terrible thing happened. You died, and I lost the letter. I lost the only written instructions for making duck the way that you did. I have all the other recipes from you that I want, but I lost your letter. I'm sad that you took it to the grave with you. I lost a memory, a precious letter from my mom, and the only recipe in the world for making the most scrumptious duck dinner.

Maybe it was appropriate. No one else should get the compliments you received. You were an excellent cook, and you deserved the praise. I think we would all love it though, if you could show up with just one more duck dinner, Mom.

Love,

Dee Dee

As I started looking forward in time, I imagined seeing my mother around me. Like tunnel vision, I thought of her in church and looked for her in the pews. If I were shopping with my daughter, I'd think what she might say that day. When I set the table with the Duz dishes, I imagined what she would serve. This is part of our healing process—to be able to involve or imagine our loved one in our lives. We are including them again in our activities and making room in our memories for their presence instead of our loss.

WHAT YOU'D BE LIKE TODAY

Dear Mom,

I wonder what you would be like today. I saw a woman in church whose face and mannerisms reminded me of you. She folded her hands politely and had mostly gray hair, styled like yours. She used plastic glasses for reading the hymns, but her voice was mostly silent. You didn't sing in church either.

What would you look like today, Mom? Would you still be skinny? Would you still wear a knit top, polyester pants and a sheer, green tinted scarf about your neck? Would your hair be very gray, having earned that color from a lifetime of motherhood?

What would you be like, today Mom? You would be ready to turn 72 on May 3, and you would have grandchildren 10 years older than the last time you saw them. You would still be cooking for Dad, watching soaps on TV, and either cross-stitching, or crocheting.

Most of all, were you still alive today, Mom, you'd be talking to us on the telephone. You still be explaining recipes to me and talking to your granddaughters about school and hobbies. You'd still have your witty sense of humor and enjoyment for your family. Well, at least most of the time. You would still be there for us, wouldn't you, Mom?

Love,

Dee Dee

LOOKING AT WHAT WE HAVE LEFT, NOT AT WHAT WE'VE LOST

Dear Mom,

One of the lessons I have taught my children is to look at what they have left, not at what they have lost. Together we share what blessings they have received and what they retain after a loss. We lose so much along the way like friends, homes, dogs, and moms. I hope my family is always grateful for what they have.

I wrote my own gratitude list yesterday in church after I saw a woman there who reminded me of you. I remembered all that I am grateful for. My list didn't include things like cars and clothes.

My list included the following:

Kim and his love

Jessica and Kelsey

Charlie, our golden retriever

Travels

Ocean sunsets

Ocean sunrises

Food and the great variety I enjoy

Commitment to excellence

Helping people be great

Helping solve organizational problems

Ability to read and learn

Ability to work out and walk

Understanding and loving friends

People with depth

God's will and vision for my life

God's Words

God's caring people

Ability to write and think

The journey of my soul

Forgiveness of sins

Vision for my life

Lifelong friends

Lifelong family

People who really care

Unselfish people

People with integrity, vision, honesty, and caring

Places to volunteer my help and skills and for God leading me to them

The pastor described faith as the ability to see the world as God intends it to be. I am grateful for many things that I think make the world the way God intends it to be. I am richly blessed, Mom. I feel like I am the luckiest person alive to be able to have love, my profession, and to live fully. Thank you for everything you did to help me be what I am today.

Love,

Dee Dee

I have said thank you to my mother in many ways through my letters. Yet saying the final thank you closes the door to the past and my grief. Mom is with me, and will be forever. I hold her memories close enough to hug now and then. My heart still aches some, and I think of her often. However, the feeling of being an orphan at the beginning of my first letter to Mom is transforming. I am growing into the woman she'd want me to be, feeling empowered by her passing and stepping into my own time now.

THIS IS MY LIFE

Dear Mom,

You died at 62 of a heart attack. Your mother died of heart failure at 62. Death cut short both of your journeys. I attended both of your funerals, and I ponder just how long I will live with this family history.

To stop this negative pattern, I am living a healthier life. I actually eat soy occasionally; red meat is an infrequent menu item. I'm up to five servings of fruit and vegetables daily, and I do an occasional glass of Chardonnay. I have a personal trainer named Kelsey who gives up on me far too often. I work out, lift weights, and am losing weight and inches despite carrying what Kelsey calls my "kangaroo" tummy.

Your early death and that of Grandma Weyer taught me more than just how to eat and exercise; I know now that I have no guarantee of tomorrow. I really may not live much past 62, if I get that far. Each day is important. Each day I have a chance to live my life fully. Even to dance.

This is my life, and it's not a dress rehearsal. A dear friend of mine survived very serious brain surgery, but she had feared she would not survive. We cried as she described her feelings and fears of not seeing her children again. Her words to me were, "Dee Dee, this really isn't a dress rehearsal." She meant it.

Life is not a dress rehearsal. This is it, and it's a wonderful dance. Whatever time I have left on earth is a blessing, and I plan to live it the way I always have. Even in high school, I said I would rather have a short, exciting life than a long, dull one. In memory of your life, Mom, I am living fully and happily in every moment. There can be no greater tribute to you.

Thank you, Mom, for this great journey of memories. It has been and continues to be one of the best parts of my life. The journey back in time allowed me to recall our life together with great joy: the fun moments, values that guided me. I pass these on to my children. For just as you empowered me, I have created and encourage my daughters. I remain a mom, a sister, a daughter, a wife. All of those roles are affected greatly by a time that was simpler and less complicated—when you were the mom, and I was your daughter.

Thank you, Mom, not just for the journey, but the wonderful life it represents. Thank you for the memories, the gifts, the awareness, and the love. Thank you for being my Mom.

Love,

Dee Dee

Conclusion

You have noticed that everything an Indian does is in a circle,
and that is because the Power of the World
always works in circles, and everything tries to be round...
The Sky is round, and I have heard that the earth is
round like a ball, and so are all the stars.
The wind, in its greatest power, whirls.
Birds make their nest in circles,
for theirs is the same religion as ours....
Even the seasons form a great circle in their changing,
and always come back again to where they were.
The life of a man is a circle from childhood to childhood,
and so it is in everything where power moves.

Black Elk, Ogalalla Sioux Holy Man, 1863-1950

Through *Dear Mom: Remembering, Celebrating, Healing*, I was able to start celebrating Christmas again with my family. When the long-forgotten memories of childhood experiences surfaced and the photos from my cousin gave me proof of childhood, I shifted from grieving to laughing. Suddenly I found what a wealth of appreciation I held. I called these memories my "gold nuggets" because I felt like I mined deeply and consistently to uncover them. These memories helped me appreciate my mother's values and strengths even more. What I call celebrating in narrative healing is really accepting the loss and then adjusting to the next stage of living.

What is the next stage of living after loss?
- Being grateful
- Making this time your time
- Being fearless
- Keeping your faith
- Finding new purpose

We have proven ourselves capable of surviving and thriving. Embark on this journey with great enthusiasm, as I am, for we have nothing to risk and all to gain. We are empowered by the strength and values of those who came before us. Finding new purpose can be the most exciting leg of the journey. I believe each of us has a purpose. Our lives are not meaningless, random acts. Rather, our lives are opportunities to create, share, love and do good.

Dear Mom is about sharing a process that worked for me and is also my way of honoring my mother, and all mothers, for their loving acts of goodness. I hope that *Dear Mom* helped you feel connected to your mother, your children, your friends, and others on this journey of healing from a loss. And I hope that the narrative healing process of writing letters enables you to mine for your own nuggets of gold. May you be forever wealthy and rich in your life's purpose.

Footnotes

[1] Gilbert, Rev. Richard. *Finding Your Way After Your Parent Dies*, http://www.bereaventmag.com/catalog productdetails.asp?WhichProduct=1365

[2] Radner, Gilda, American Comedian, 1946-1989, http://www.insprirationpeak.com/endingsand beginnings.html

[3] http://gardendigest.com/time.htm

[4] http://www.blossomswap.com/gardens/flamingos.html

About the Author

Dee Dee Raap is an author, motivational speaker and business consultant with 21 years of experience working in media, travel, banking and marketing. Dee Dee founded JourneyWorks, a speaking and business consulting firm, in 1996, and since then, has spoken to groups across America on communication, customer care, teamwork and leadership.

Dee Dee believes in volunteer work, and has served on committees and boards for non-profits including United Way of Larmie County, Cheyenne Symphony Orchestra, and the Greater Cheyenne Area Chamber of Commerce. Dee Dee is a Distinguished Toastmaster and member of the National Speakers Association. She lives in Sioux Falls, South Dakota.

For more information on speaking engagements, special discounts for bulk purchases or for personally signed gift copies of *Dear Mom: Remembering, Celebrating, Healing,* pleaste contact Dee Dee at:

Dee Dee Raap
4015 S. Brady Court
Sioux Falls, SD 57103
605-371-2299
deedee@deedeeraap.com
www.deedeeraap.com